Bad Losers

By Brian Busselle & Nick Baker

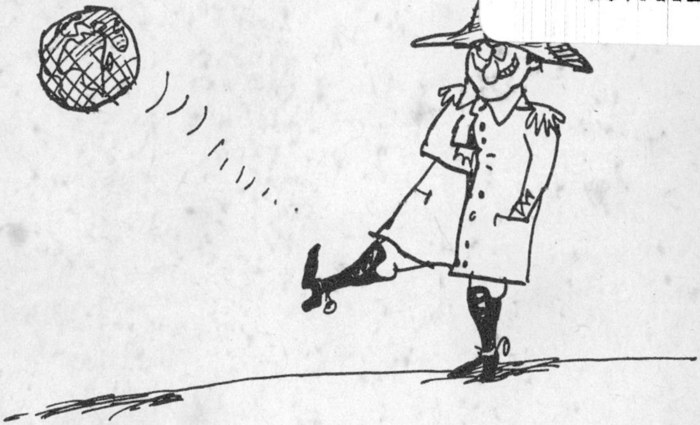

SPHERE

SPHERE BOOKS LIMITED
London & Sydney

First published in Great Britain by Sphere Books Ltd 1984
30–32 Gray's Inn Road, London WC1X 8JL
Copyright © 1984 by Brian Busselle and Nick Baker
Reprinted 1984

To Angie and Jill

TRADE
MARK

This book is sold subject to the condition that
it shall not, by way of trade or otherwise, be lent,
re-sold, hired out or otherwise circulated without
the publisher's prior consent in any form of
binding or cover other than that in which it is
published and without a similar condition
including this condition being imposed on the
subsequent purchaser.

Reproduced, printed and bound in Great Britain by
Hazell Watson & Viney Limited,
Aylesbury, Bucks

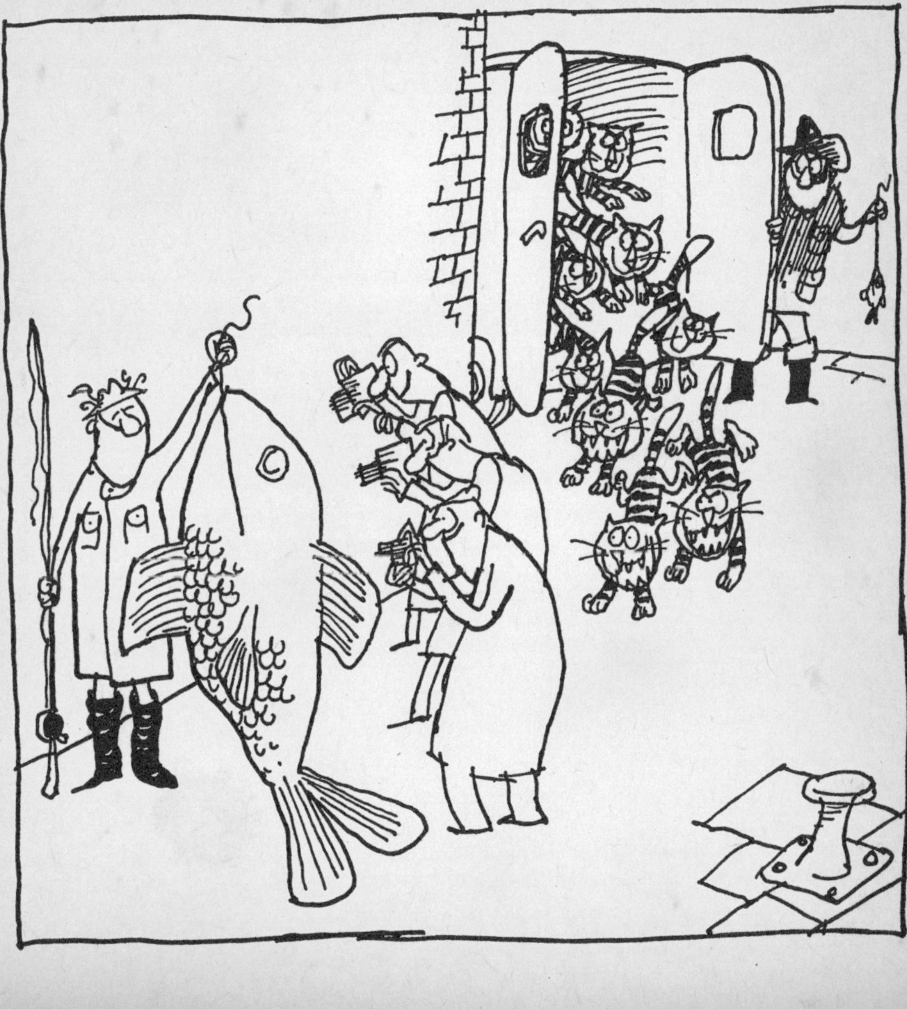

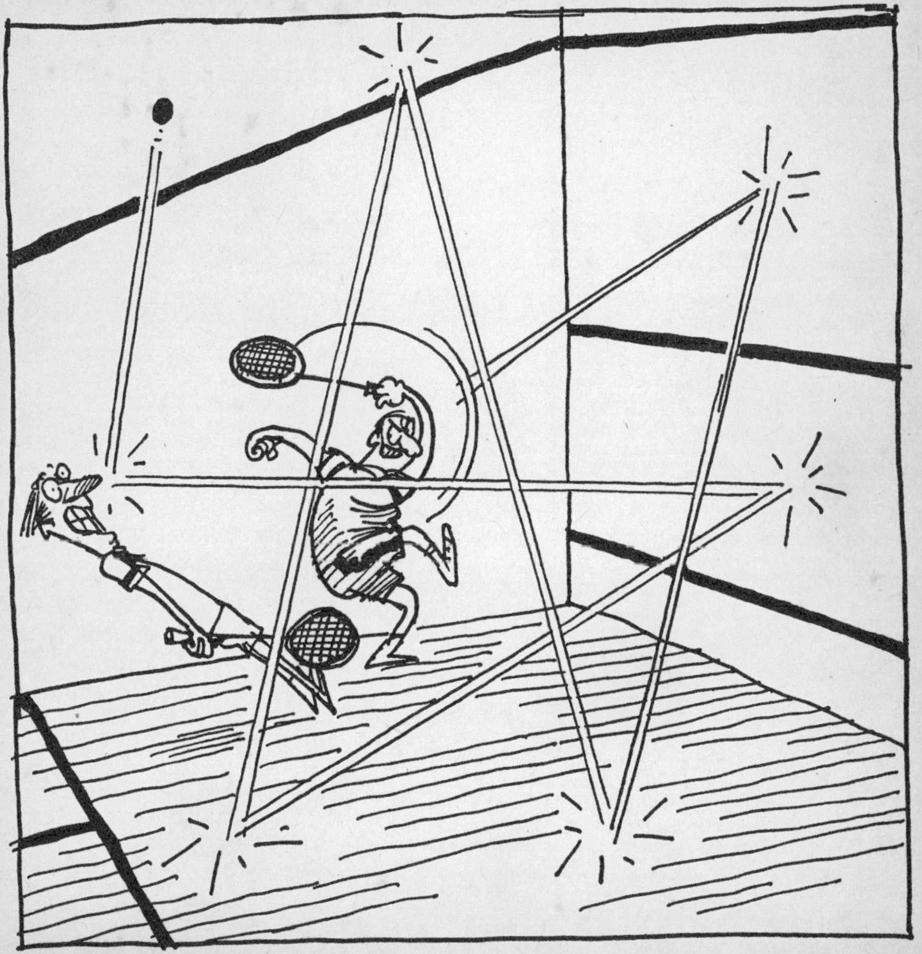

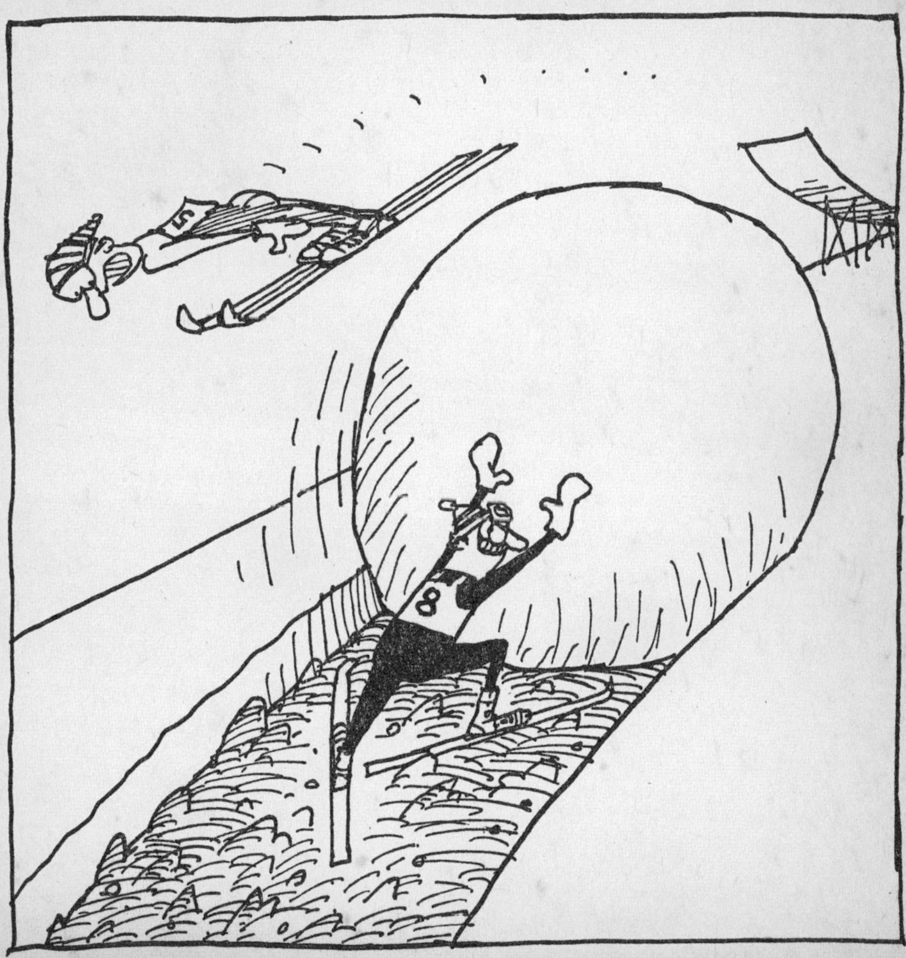

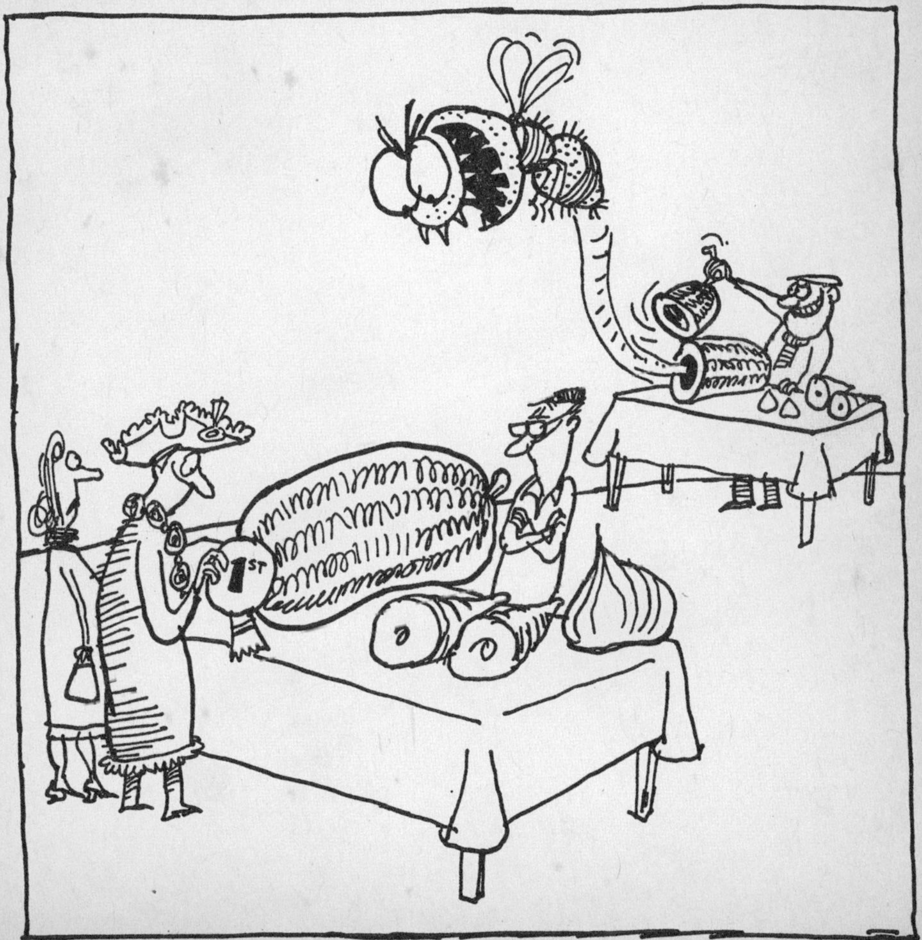
1ST

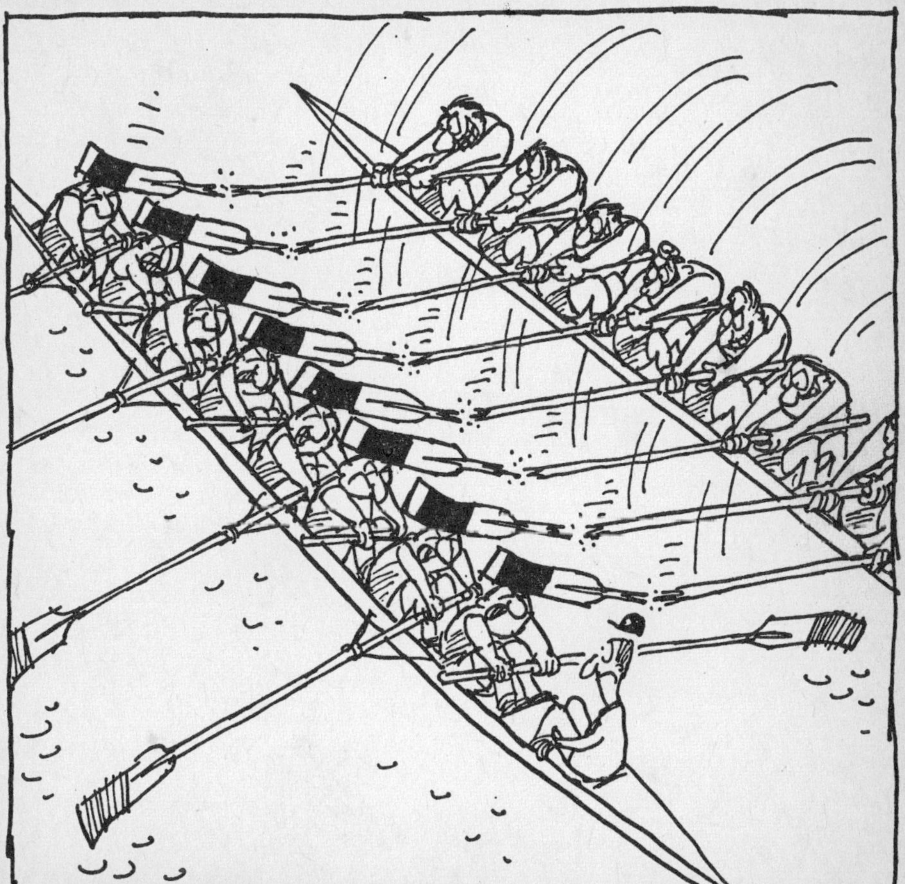

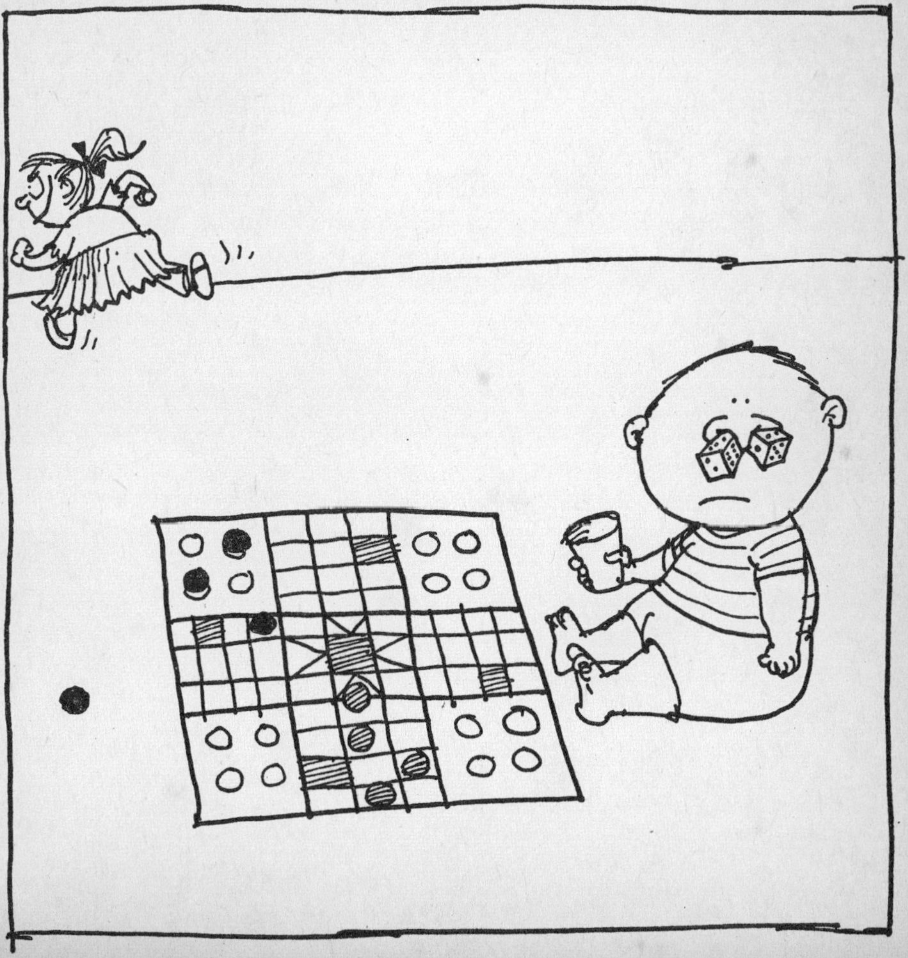

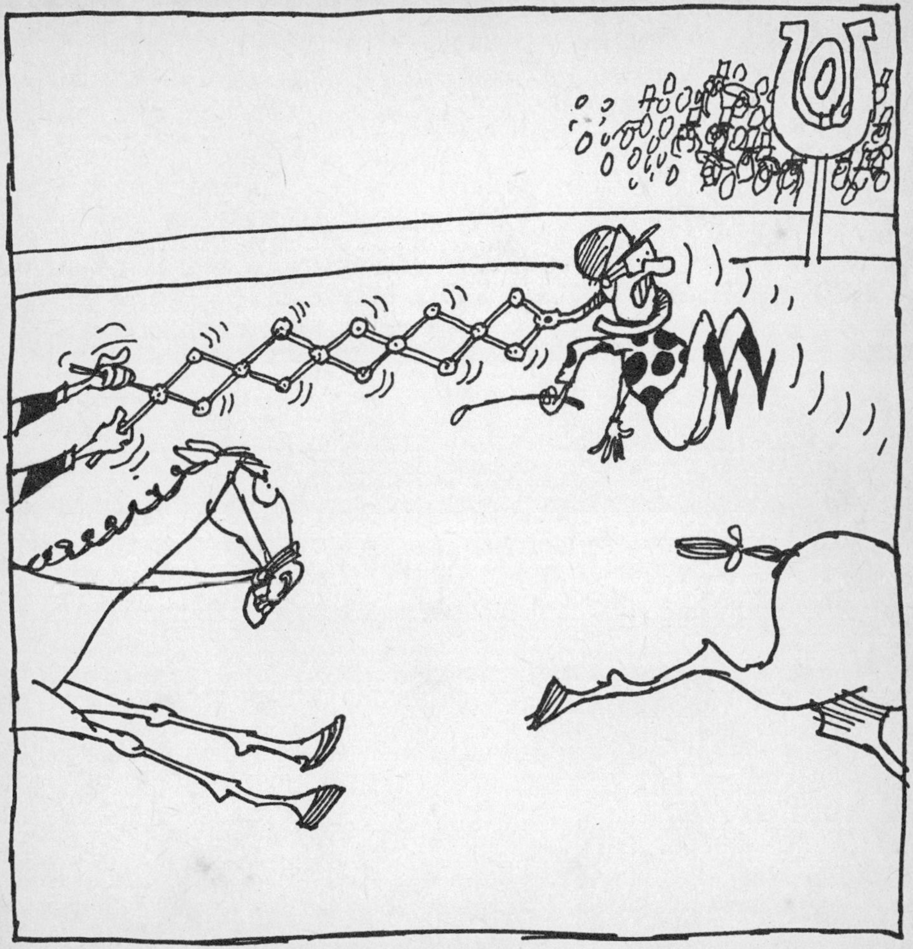

B.L.—2

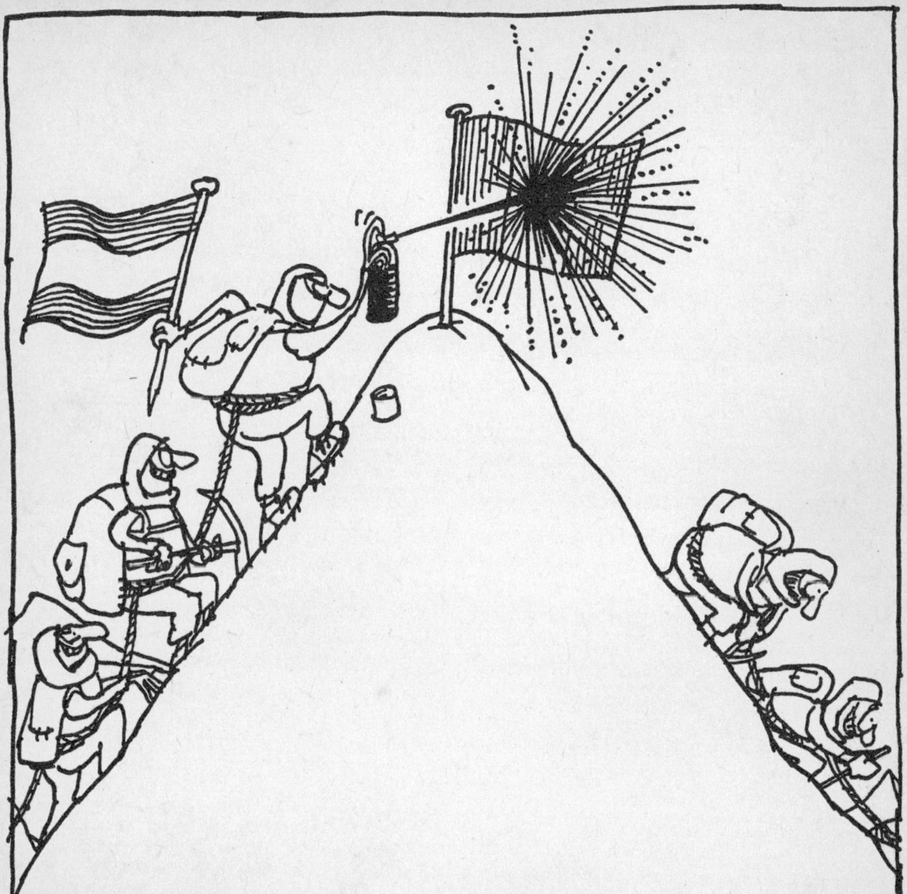

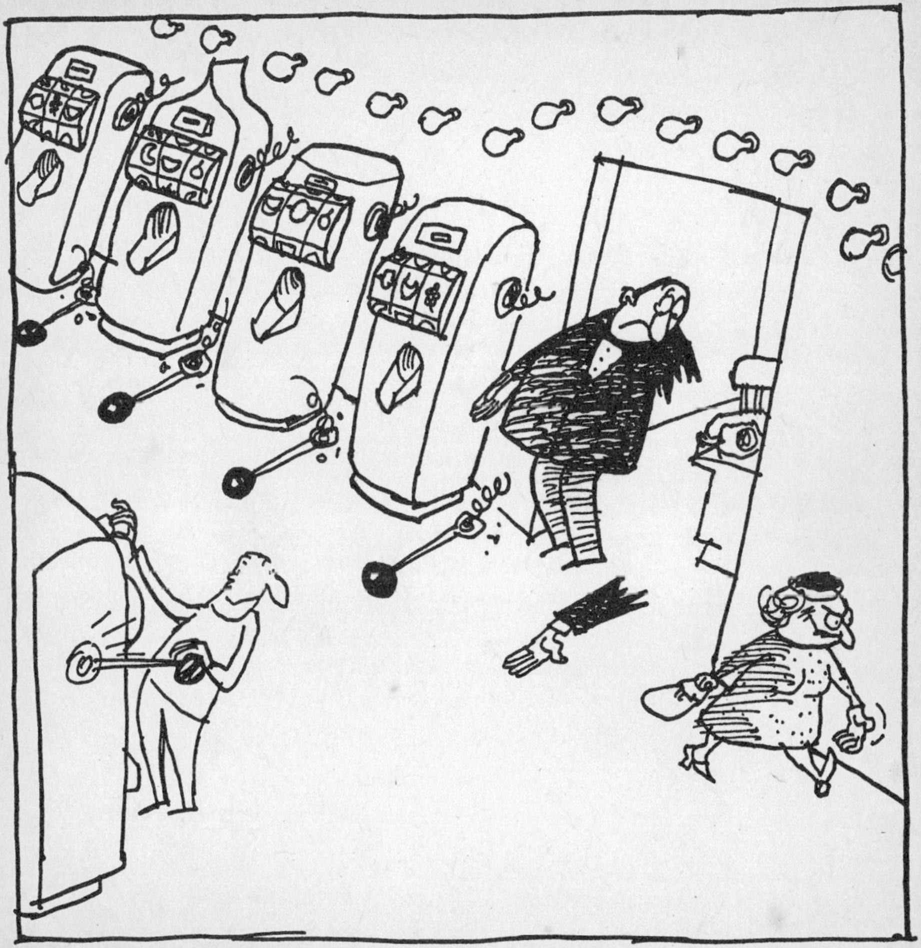

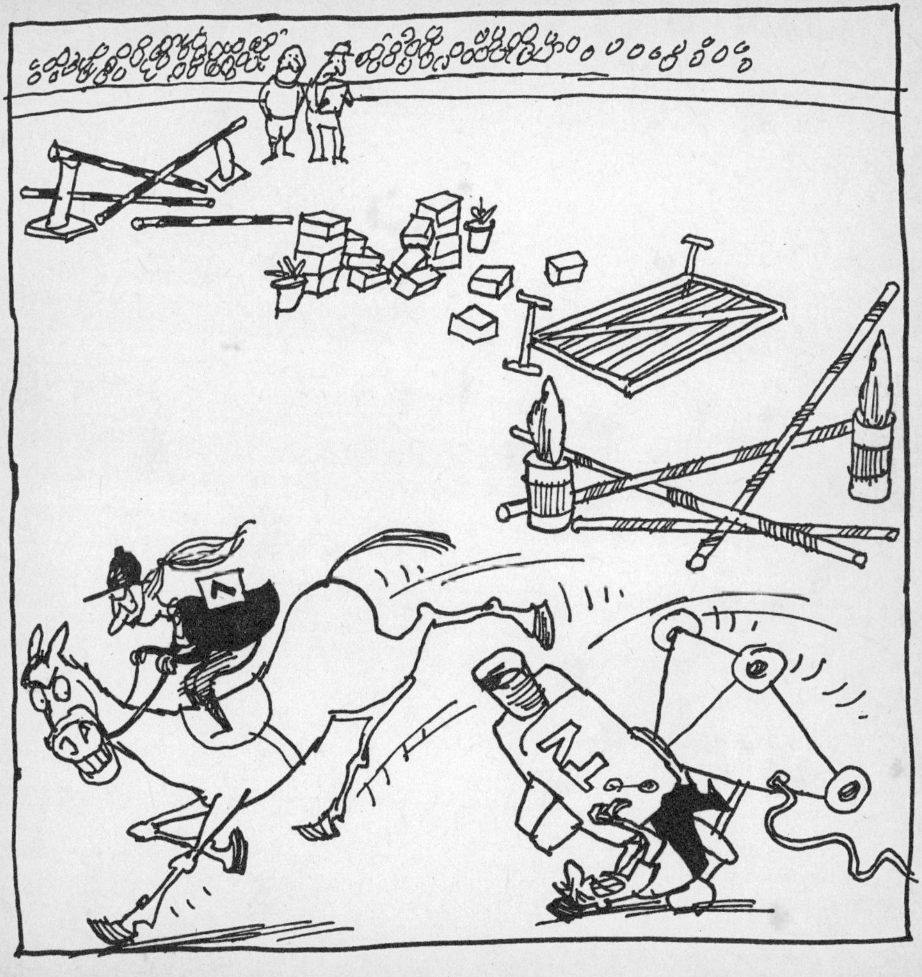
TV

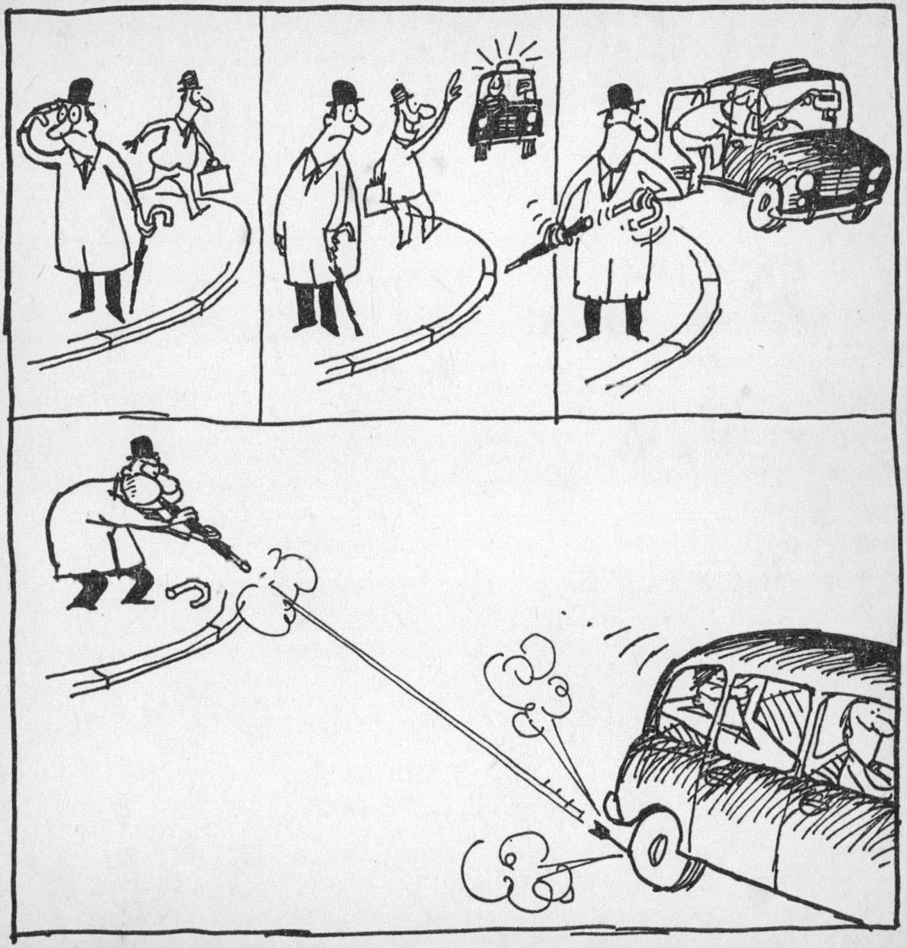

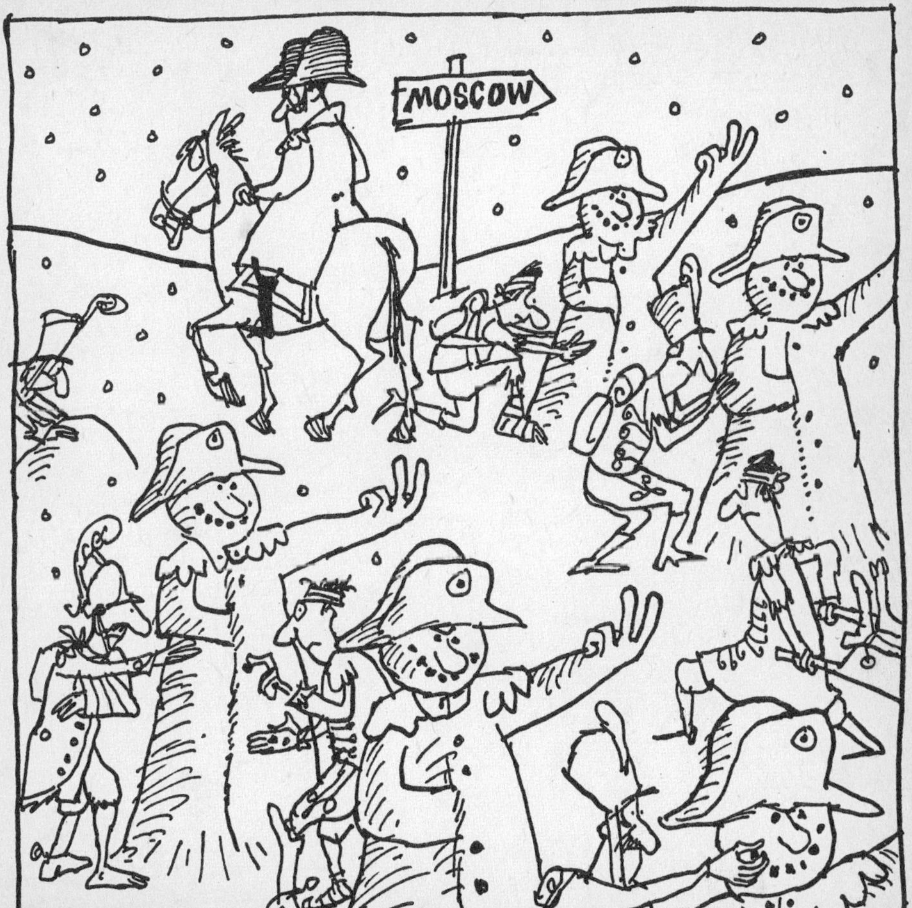
MOSCOW

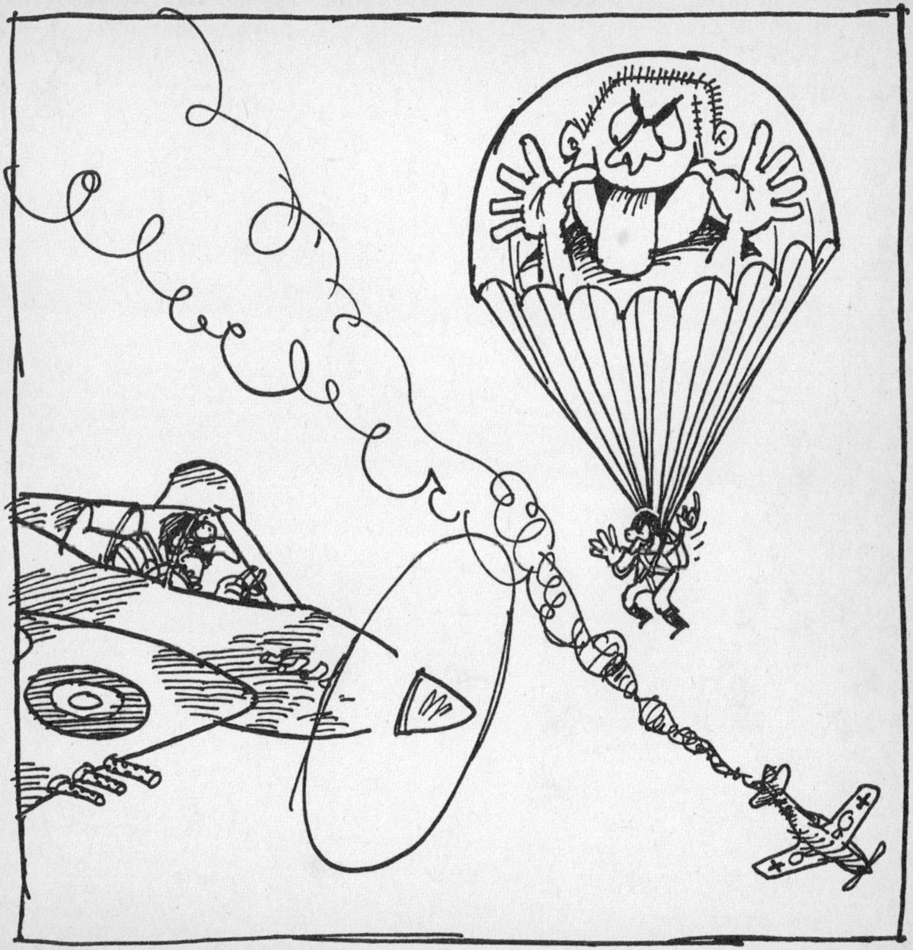

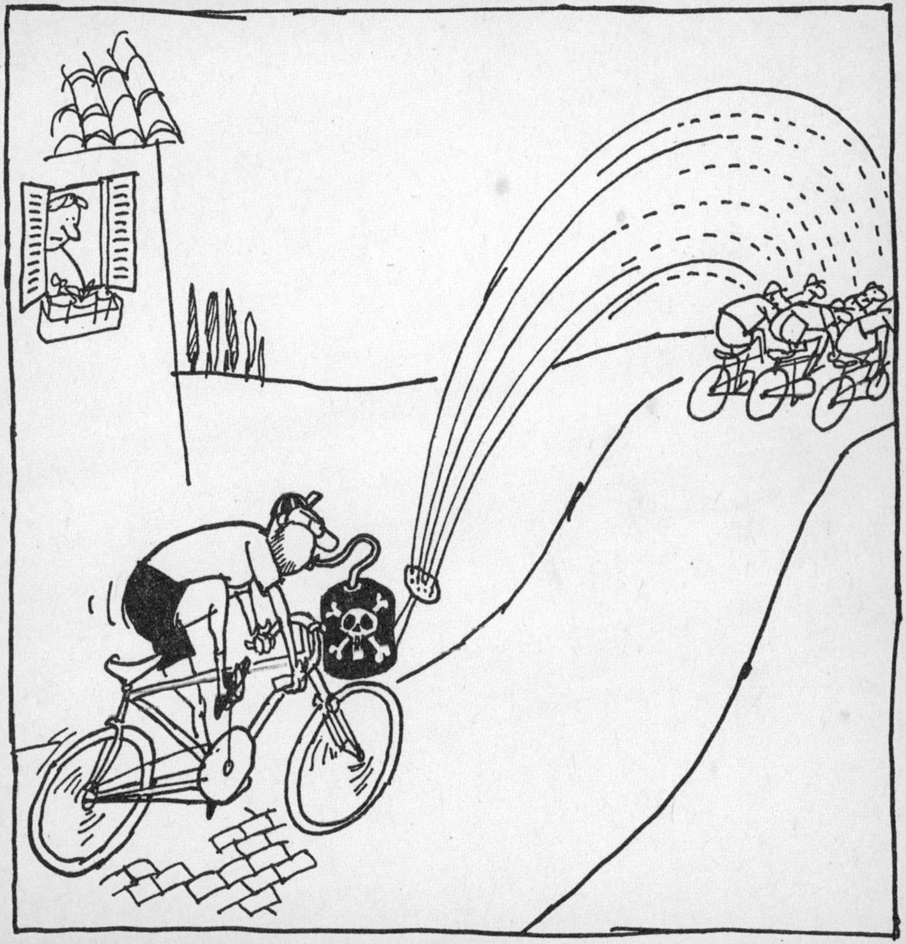

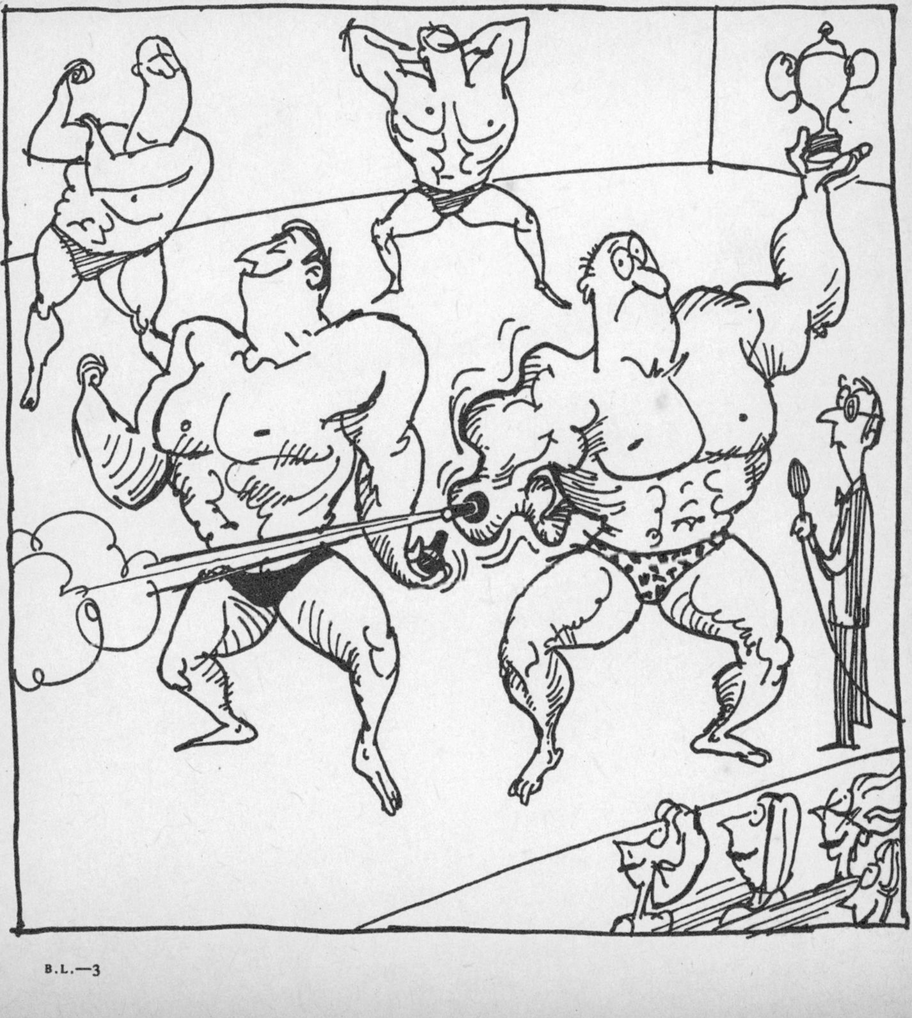

B.L.—3

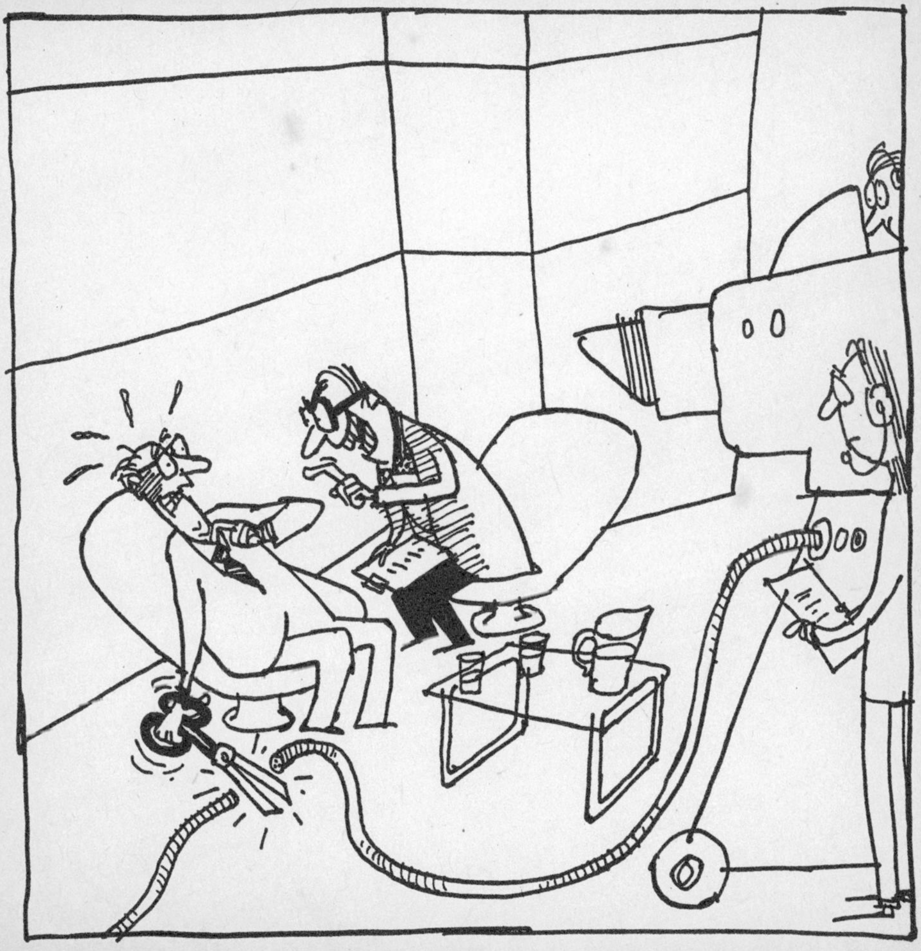

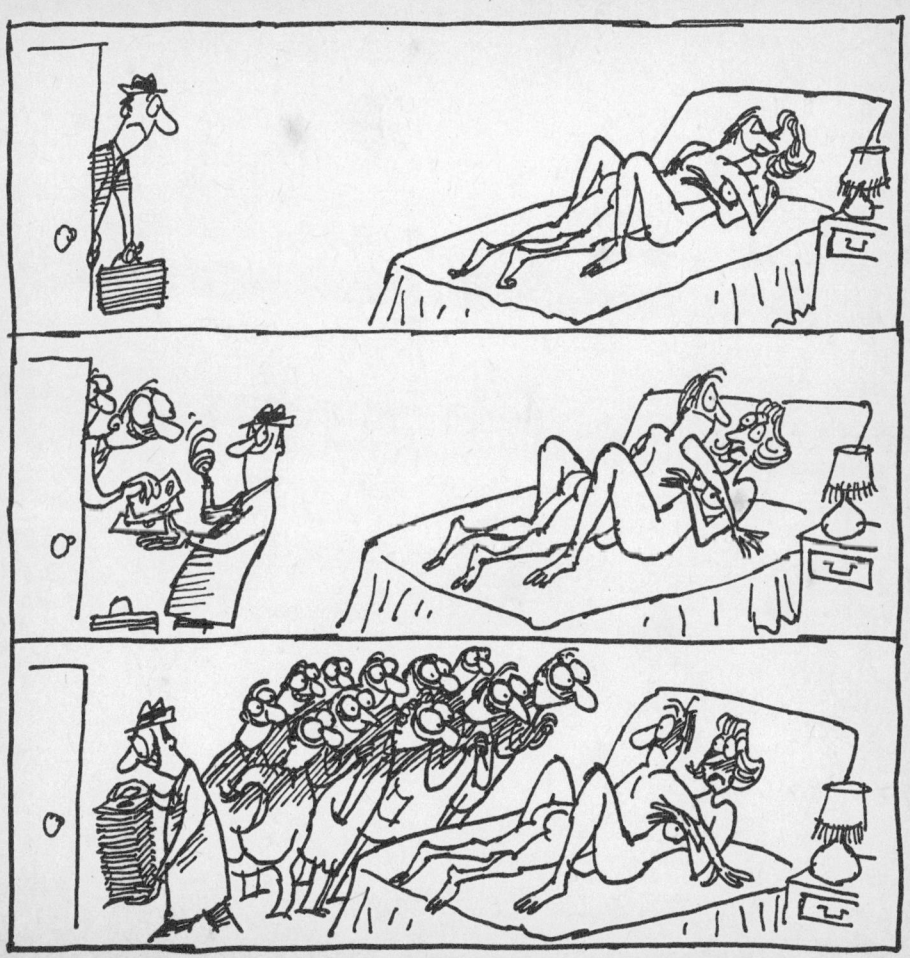

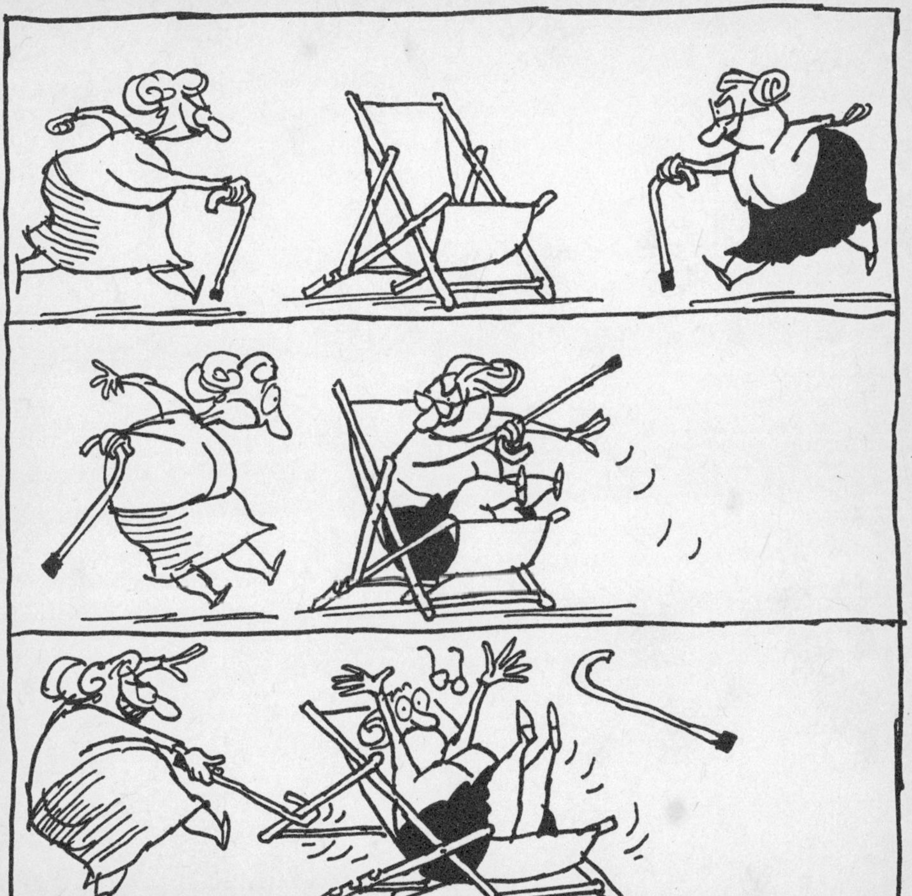

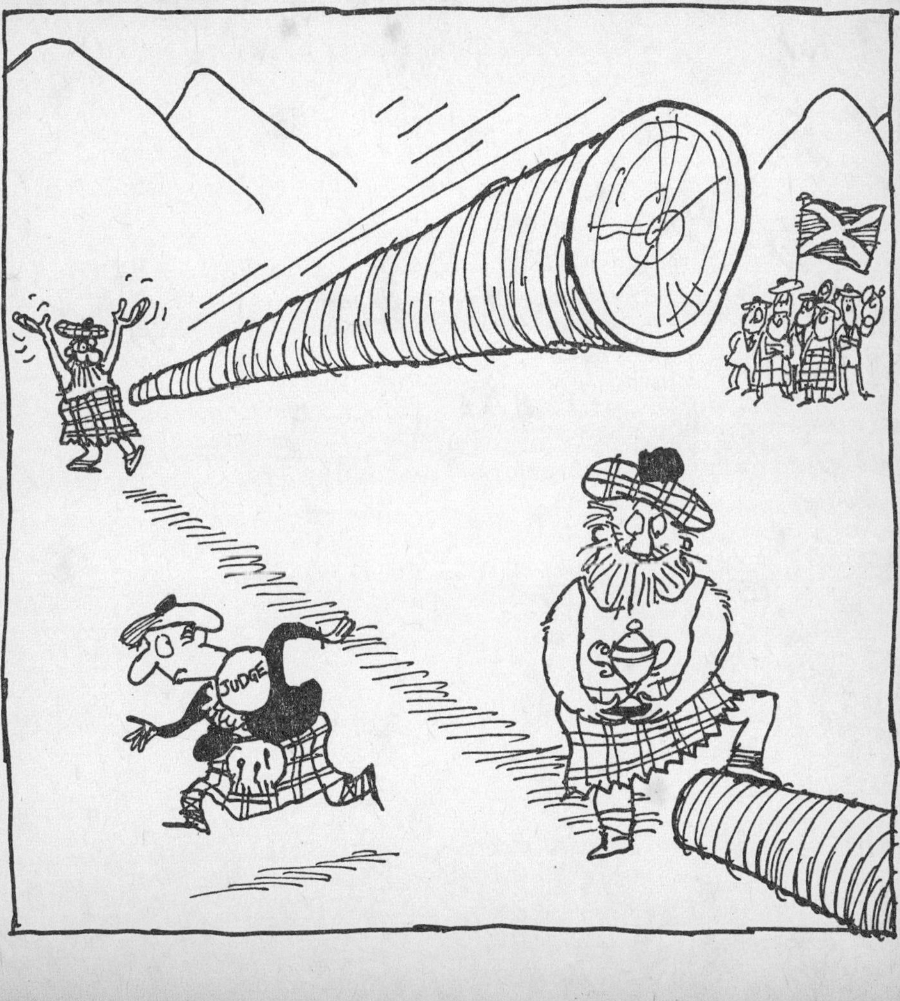
JUDGE

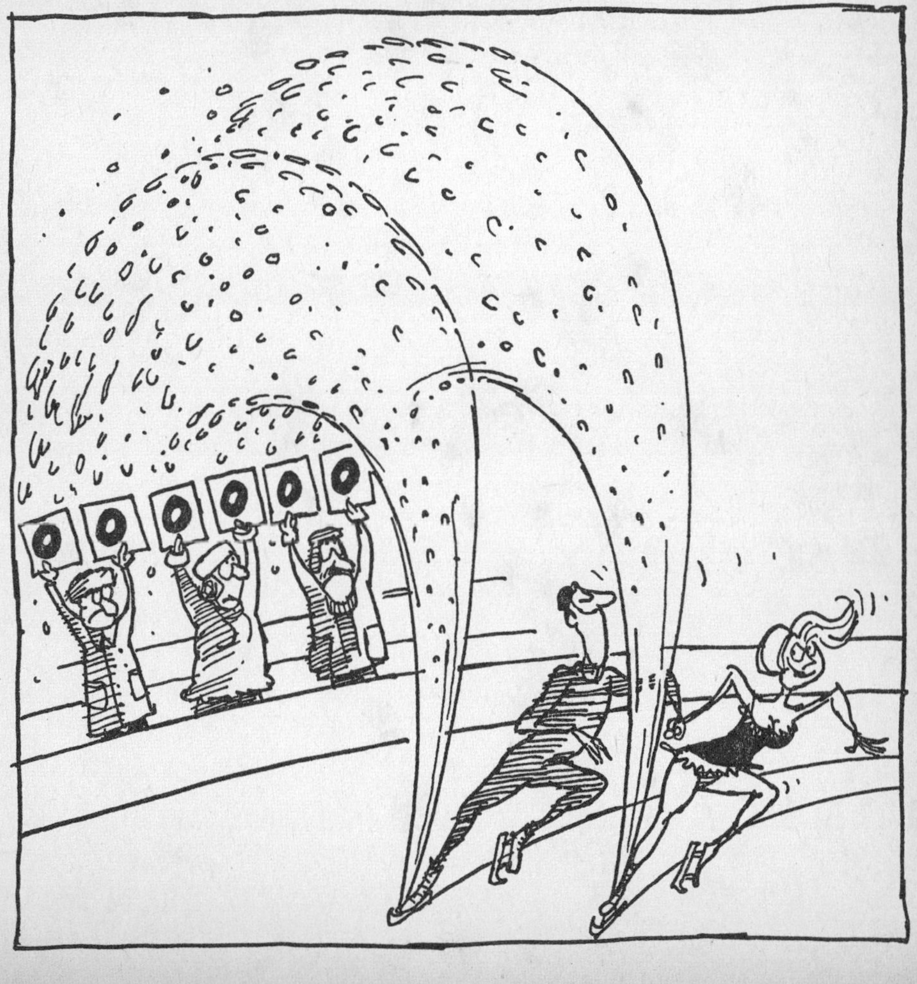

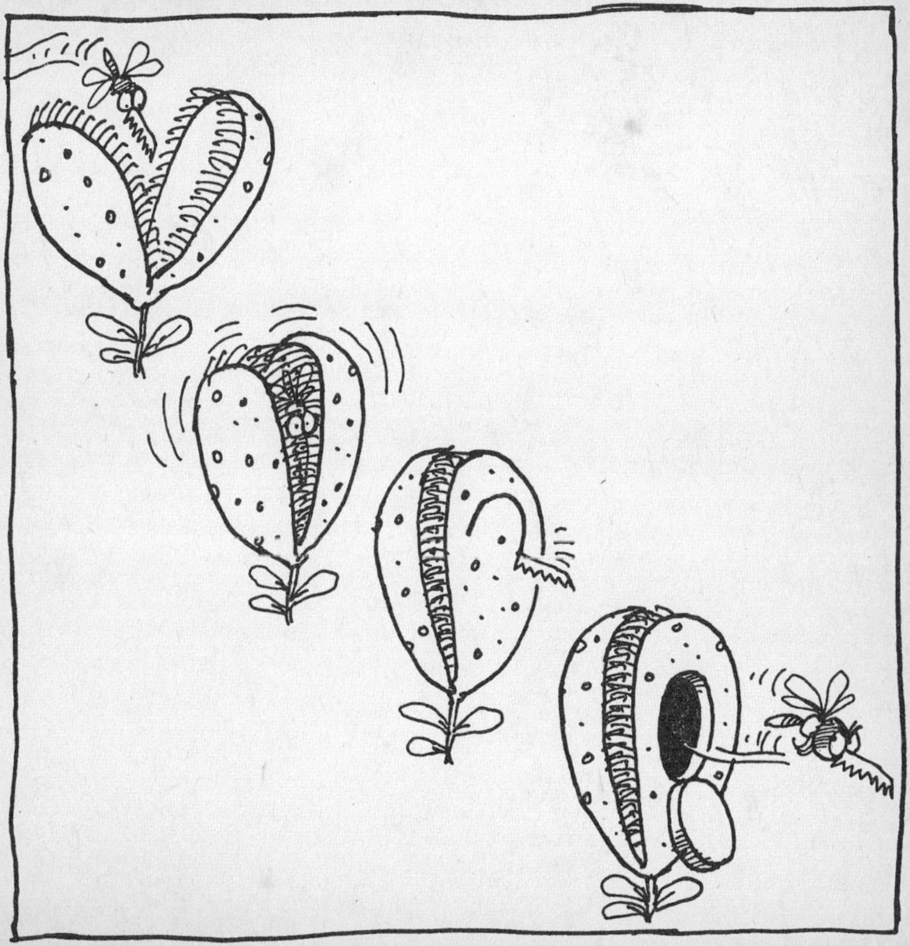

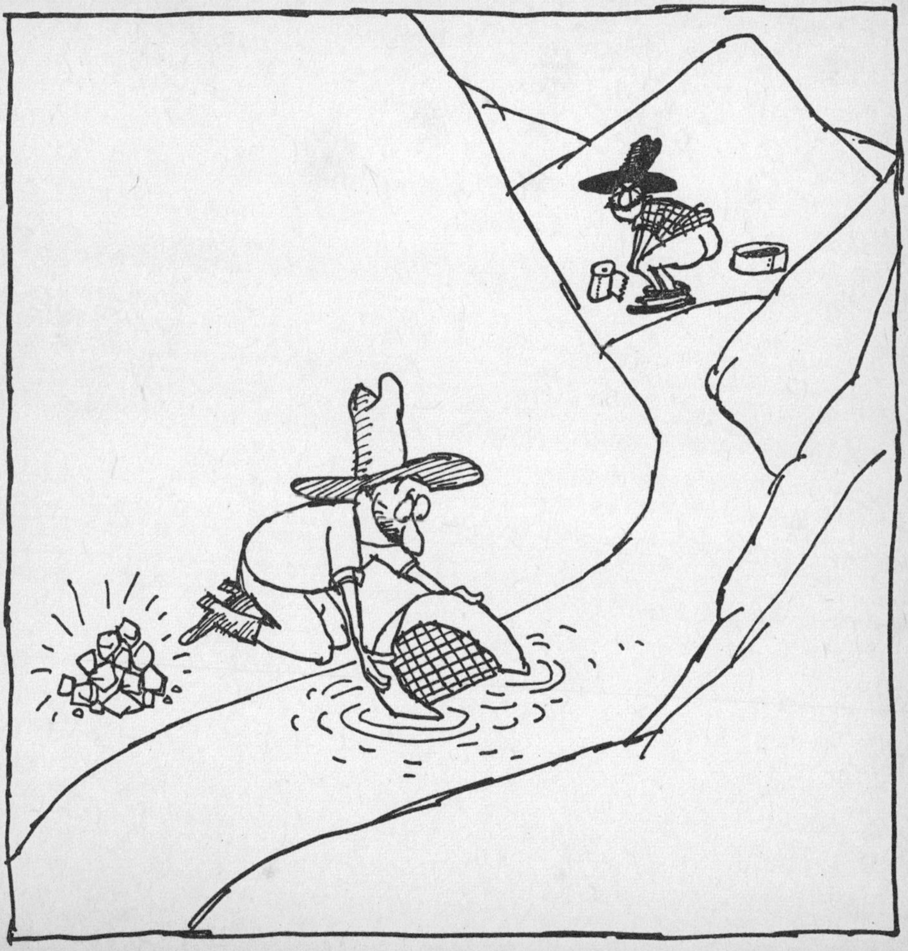

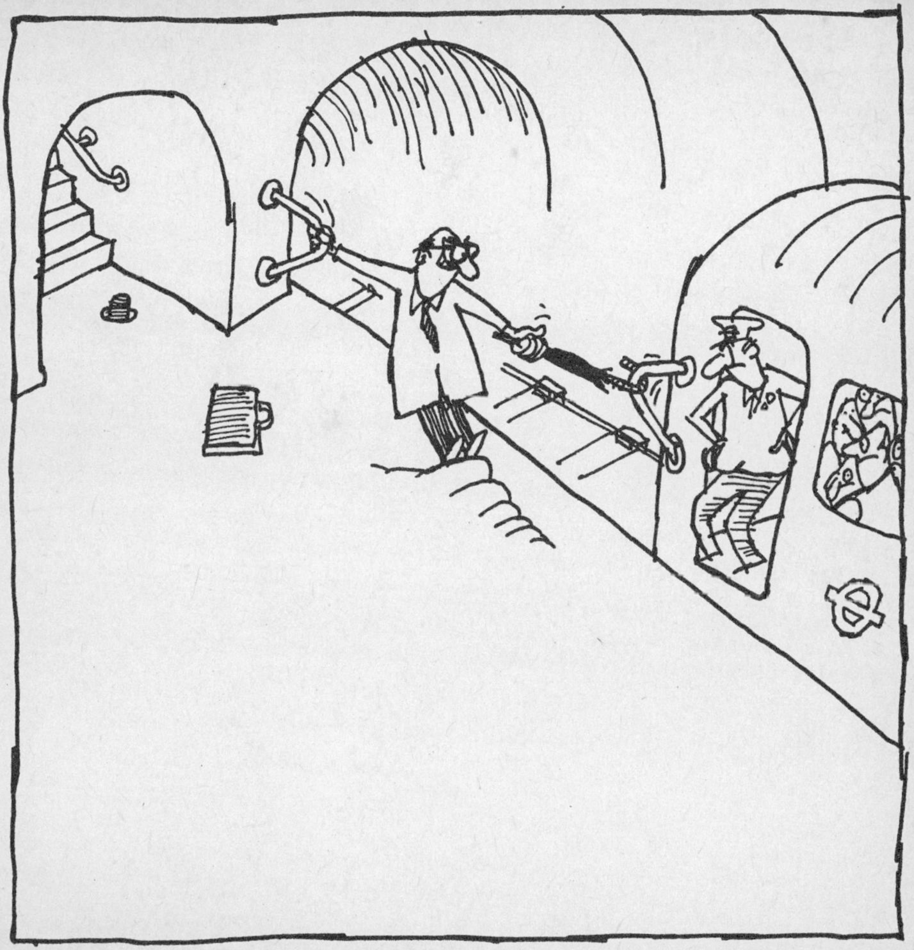

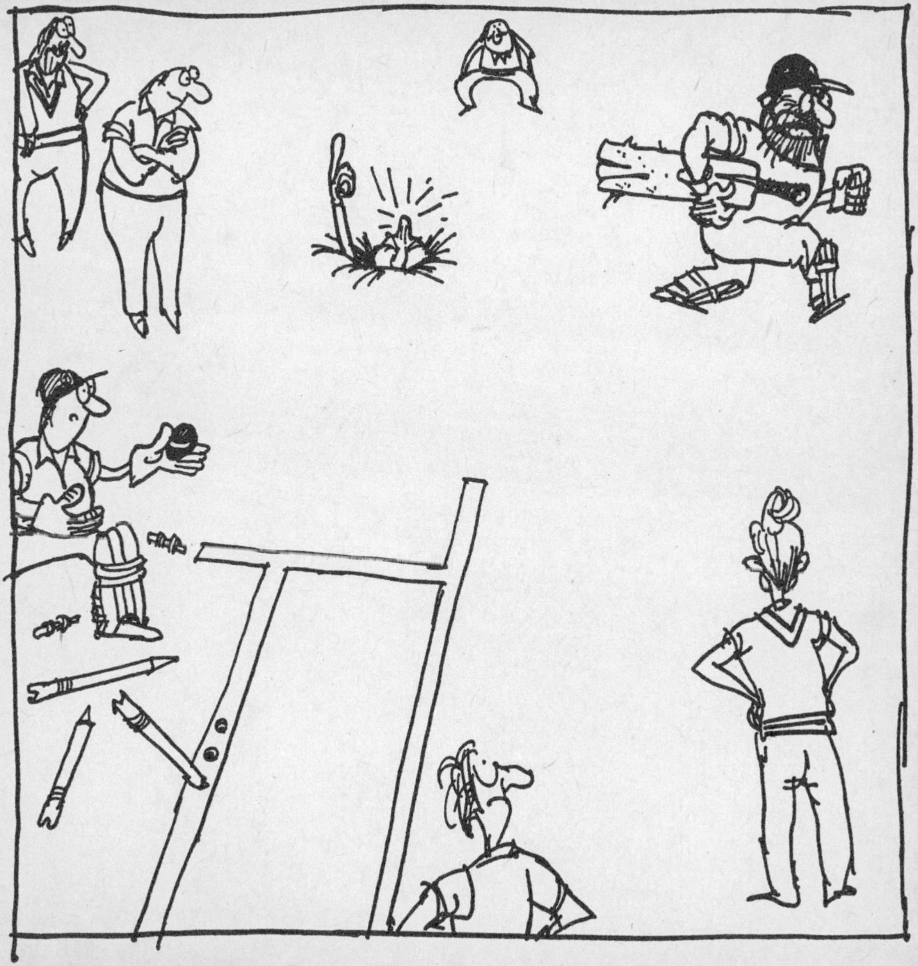

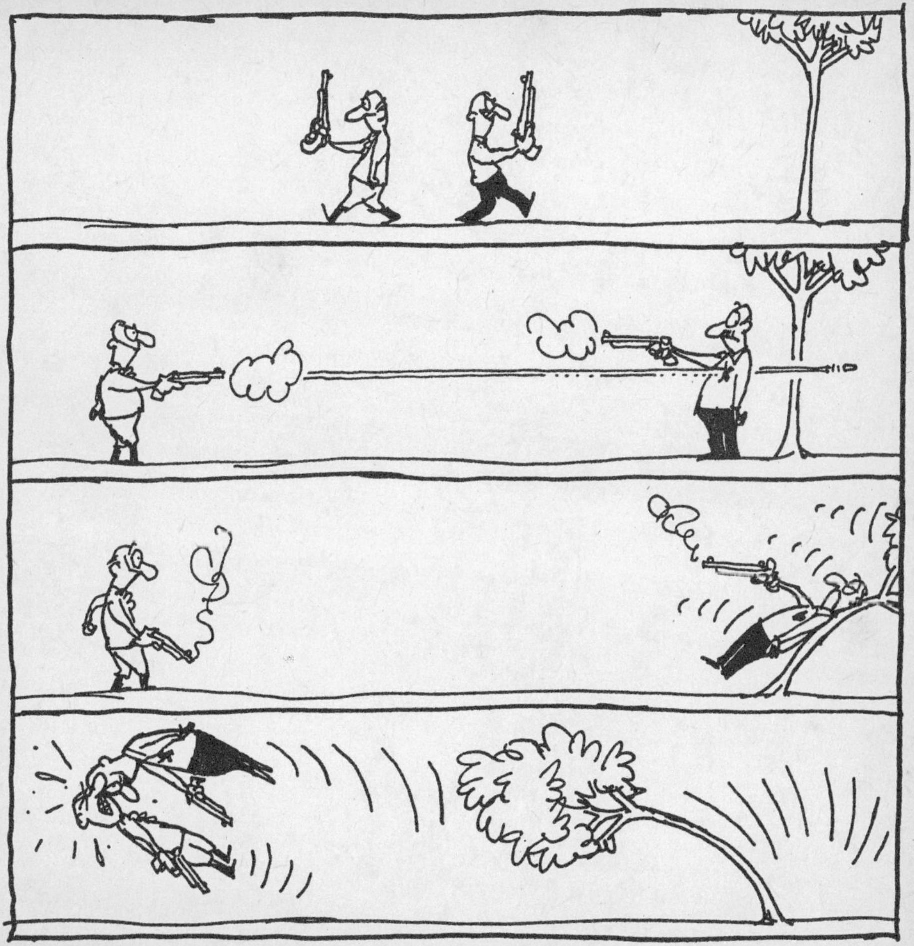

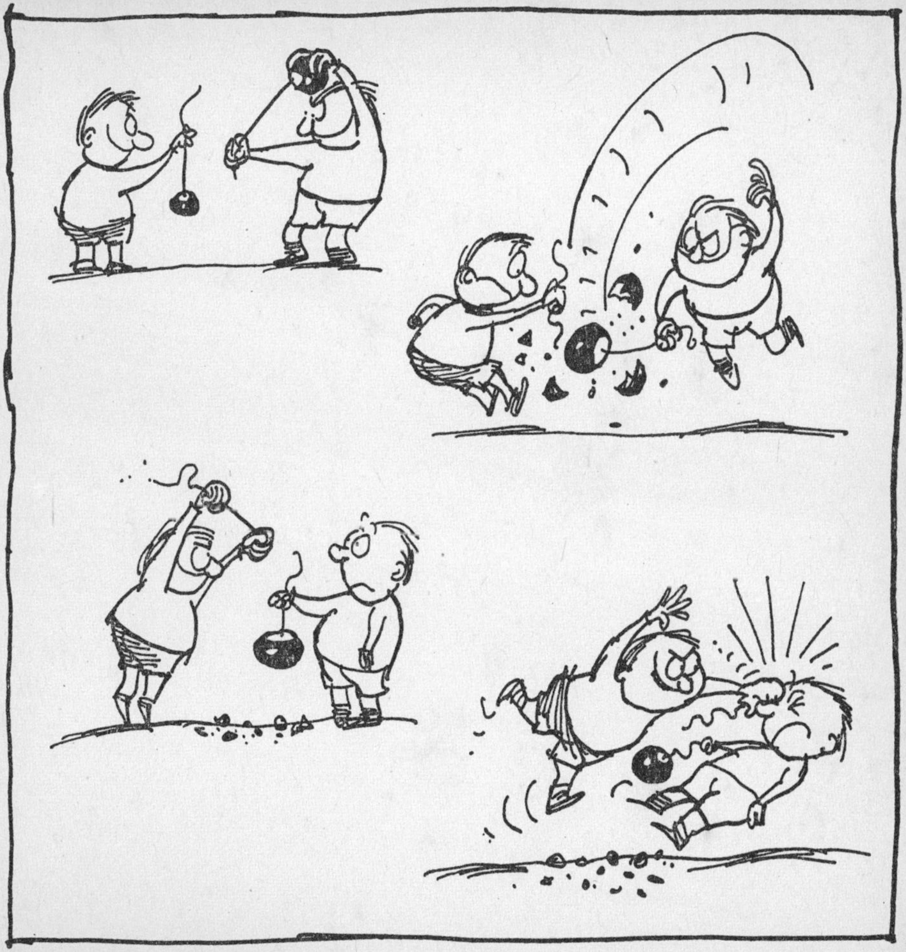

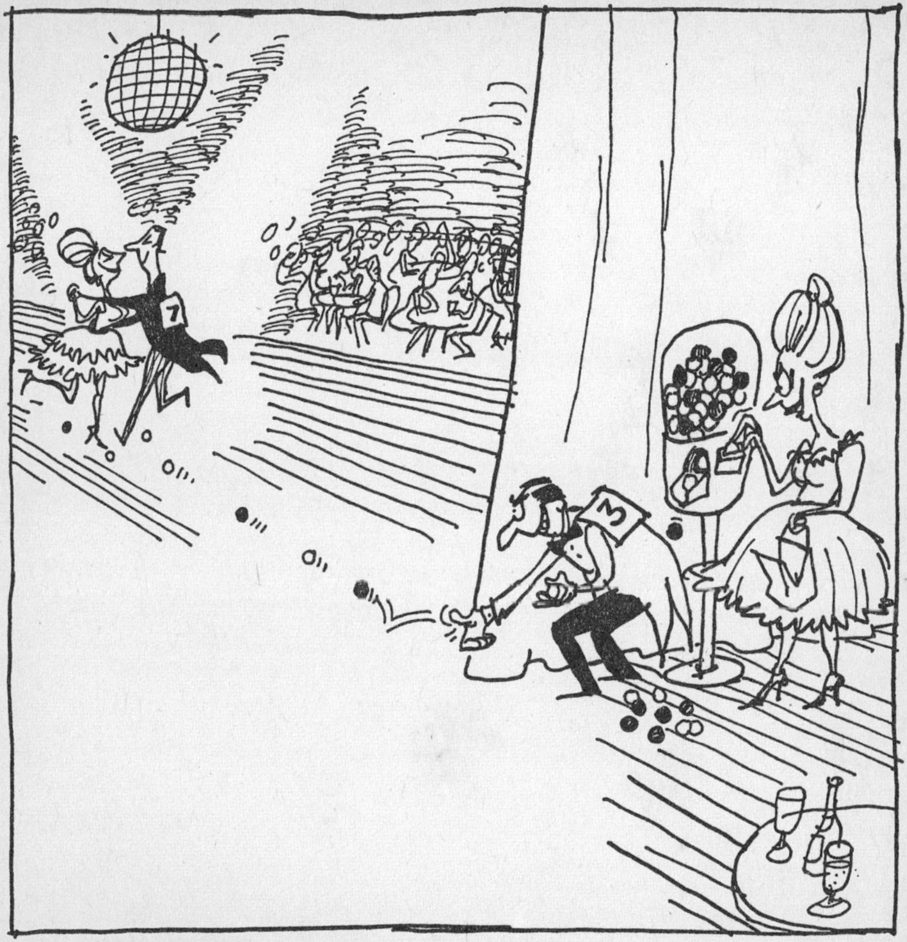
7
3

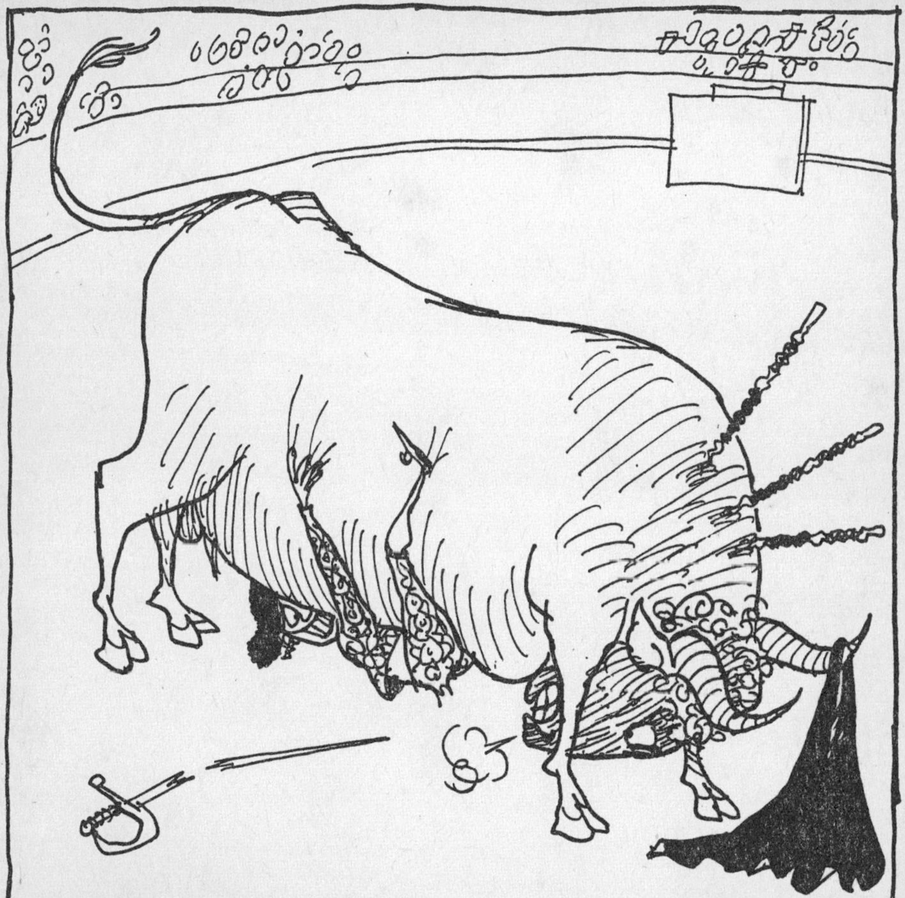

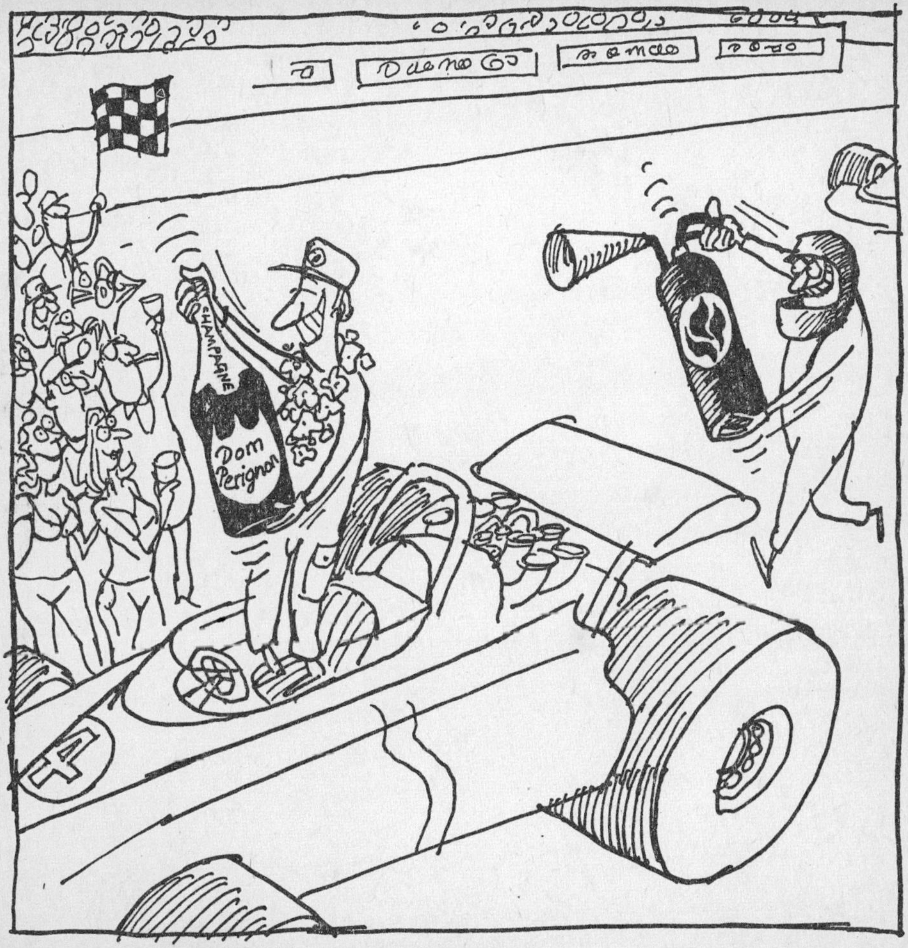
CHAMPAGNE
Dom Perignon
4

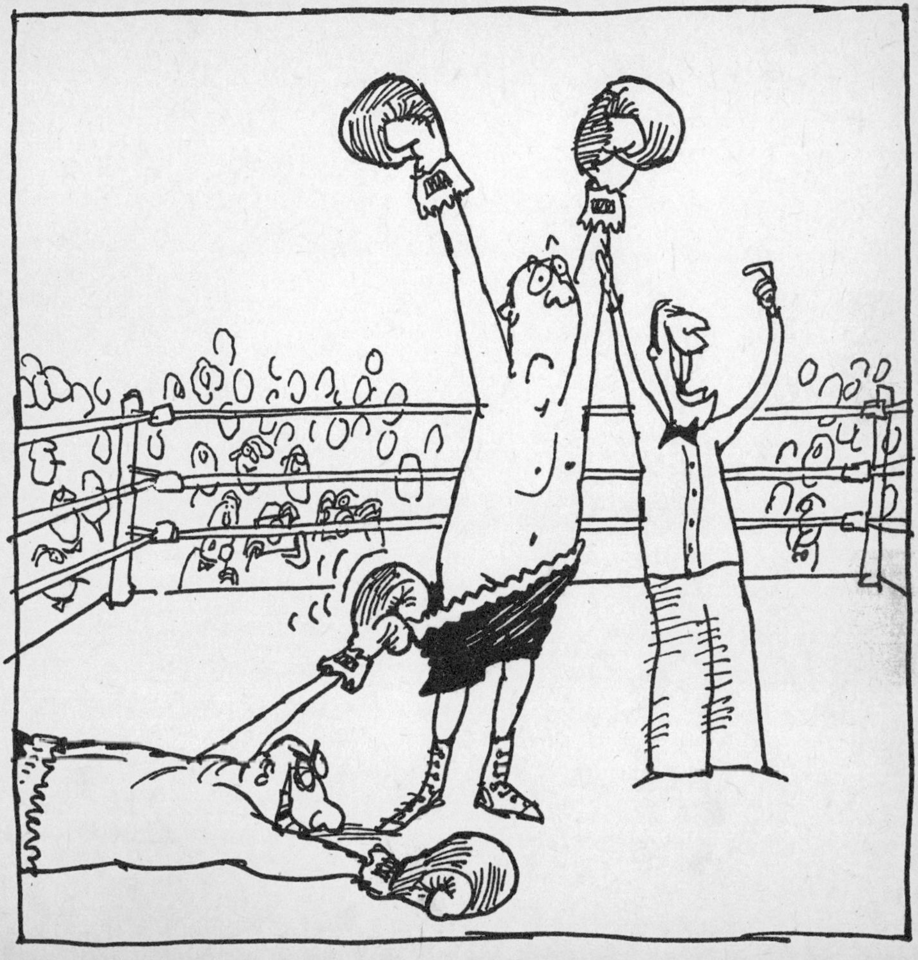

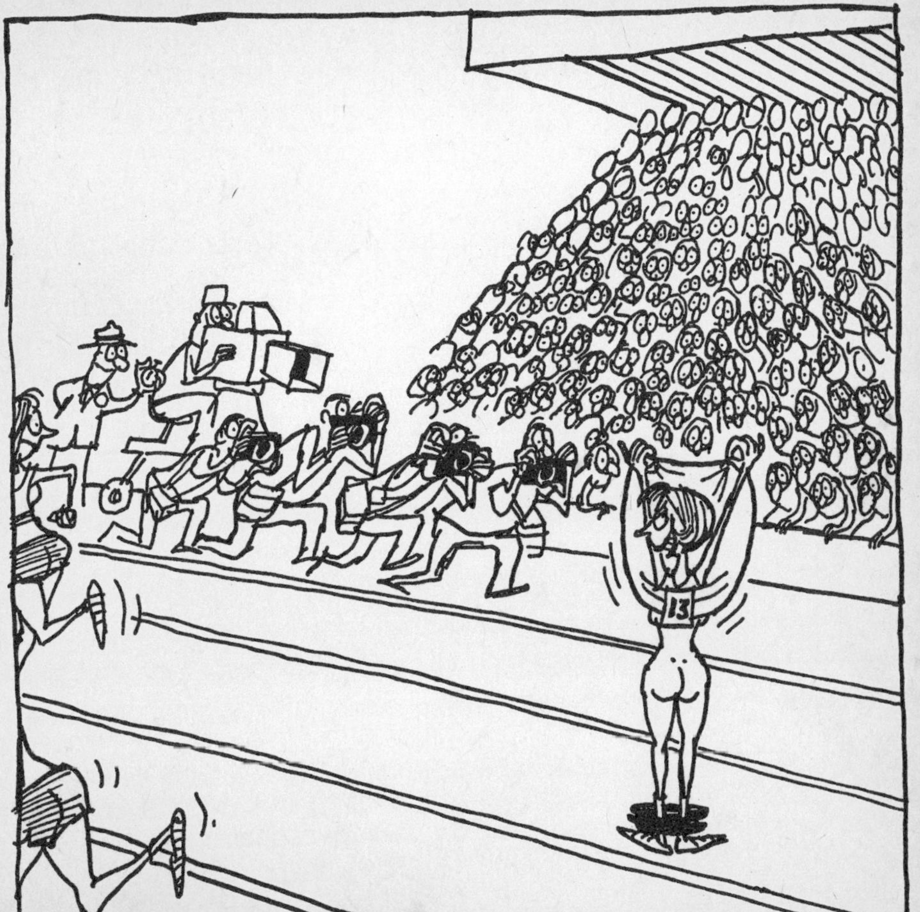
13

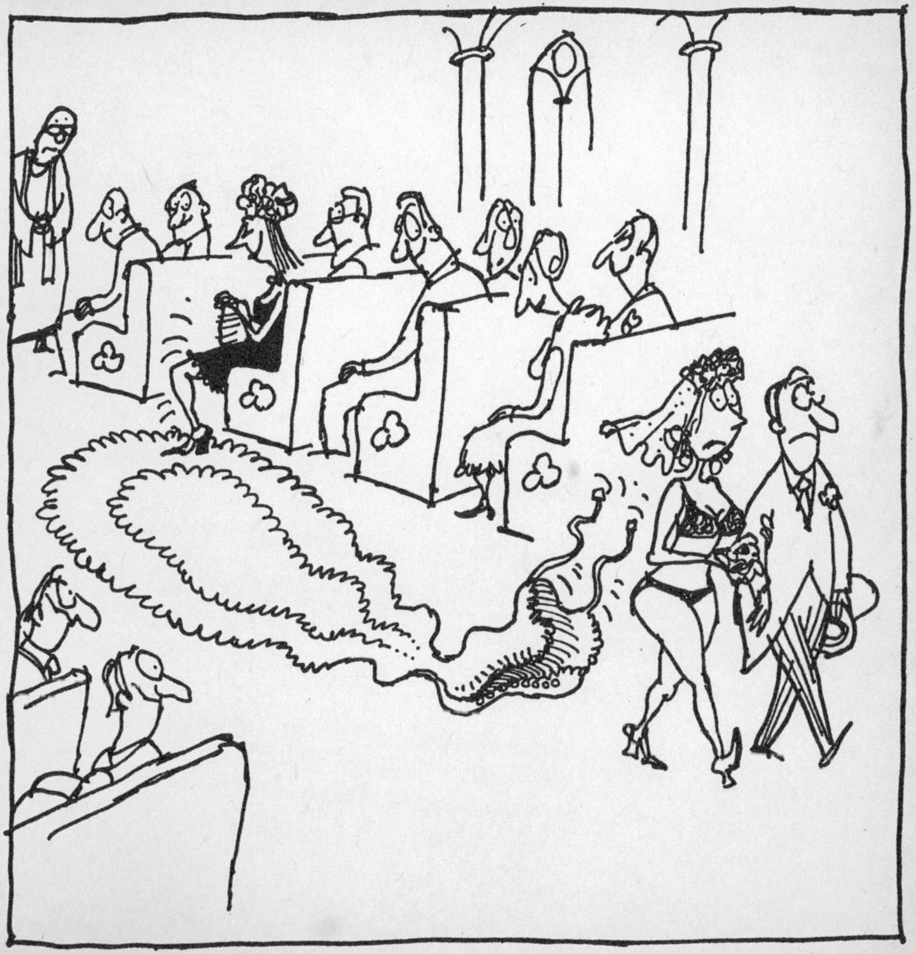

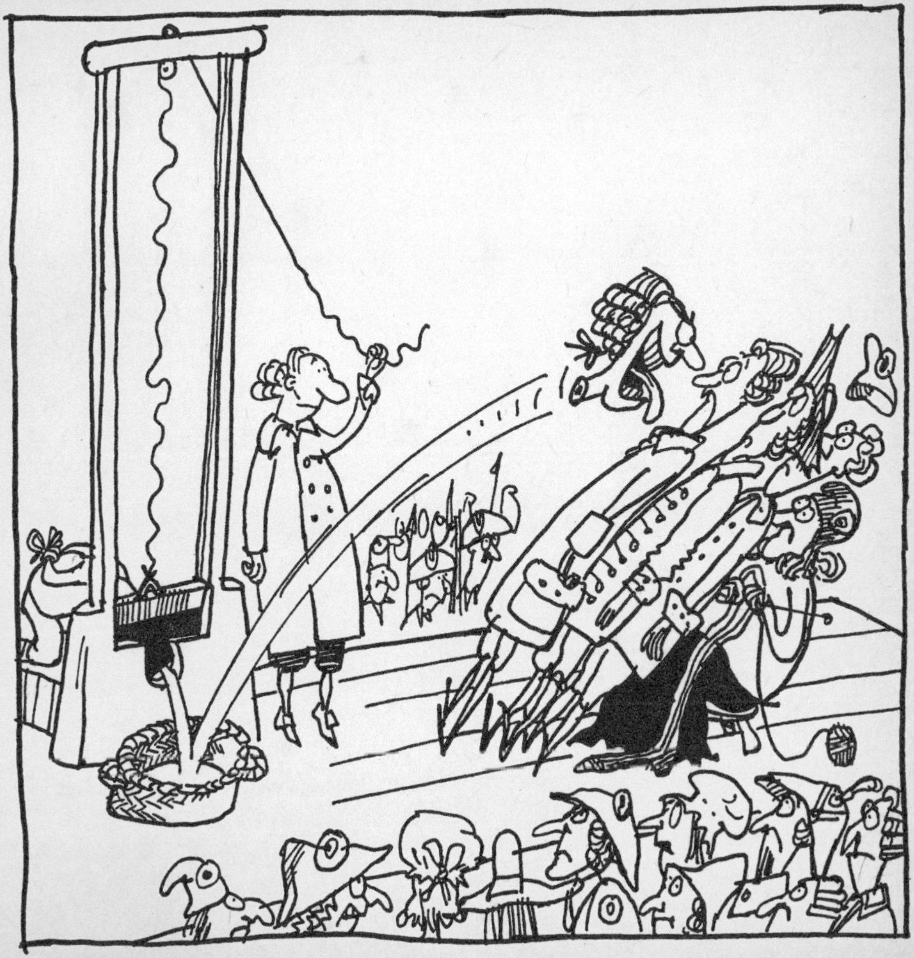

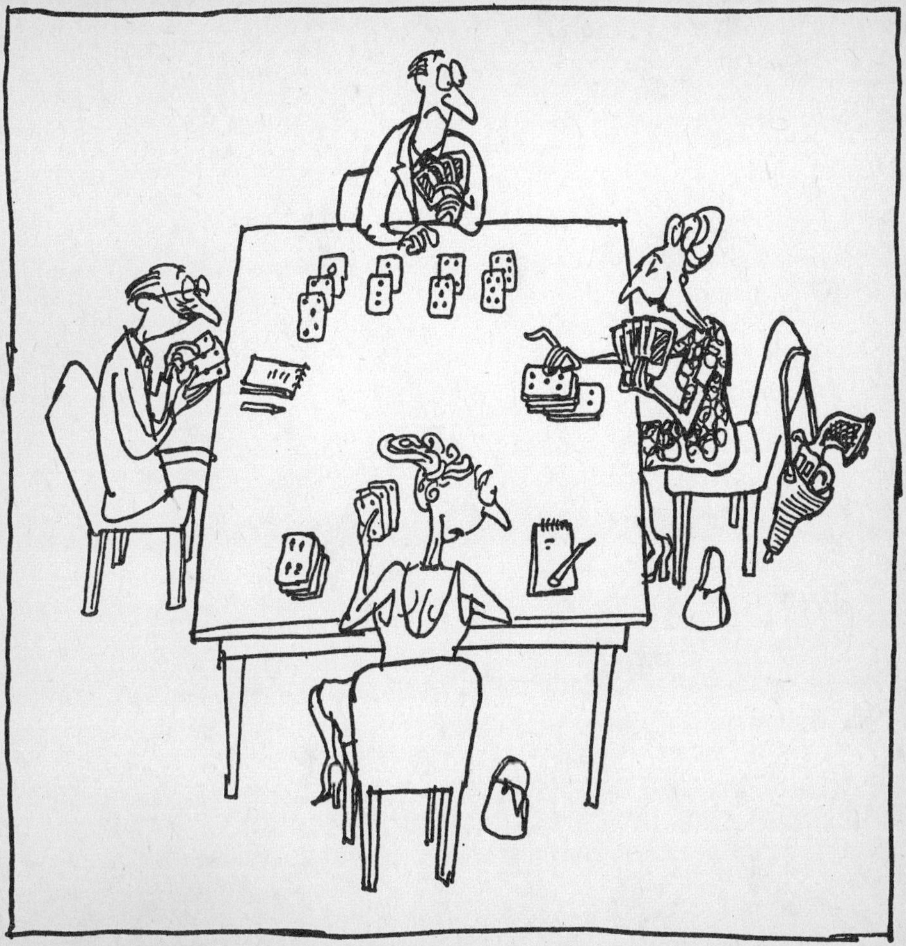

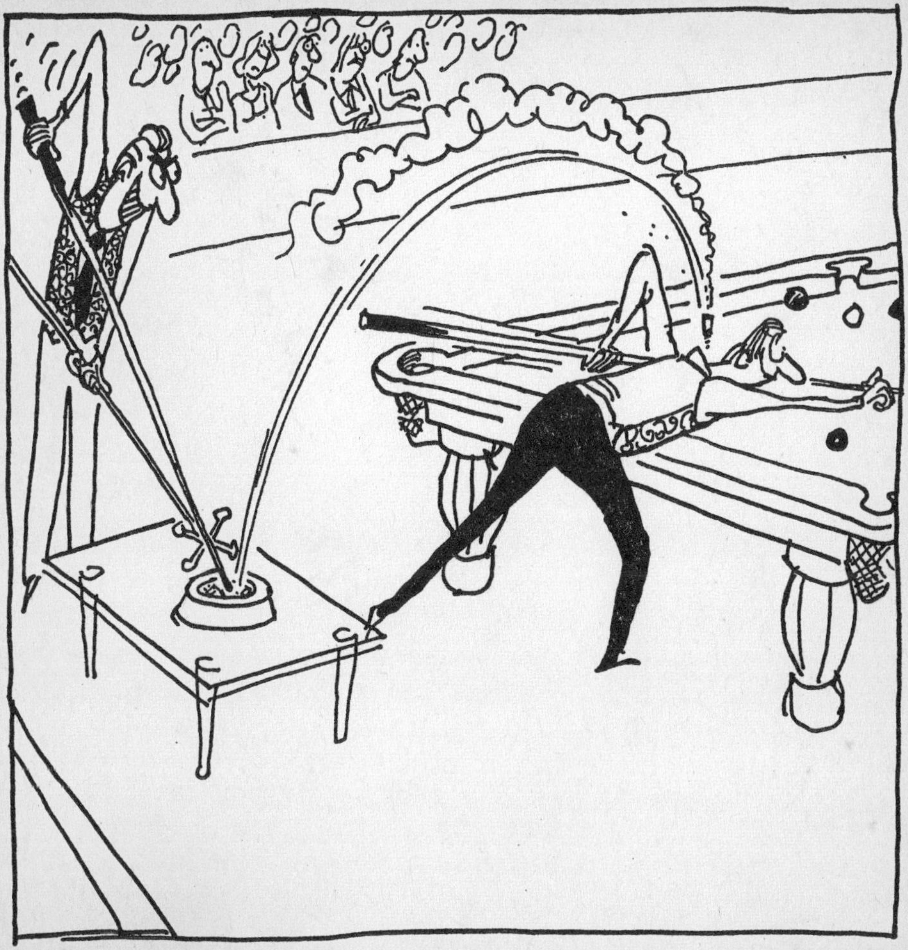

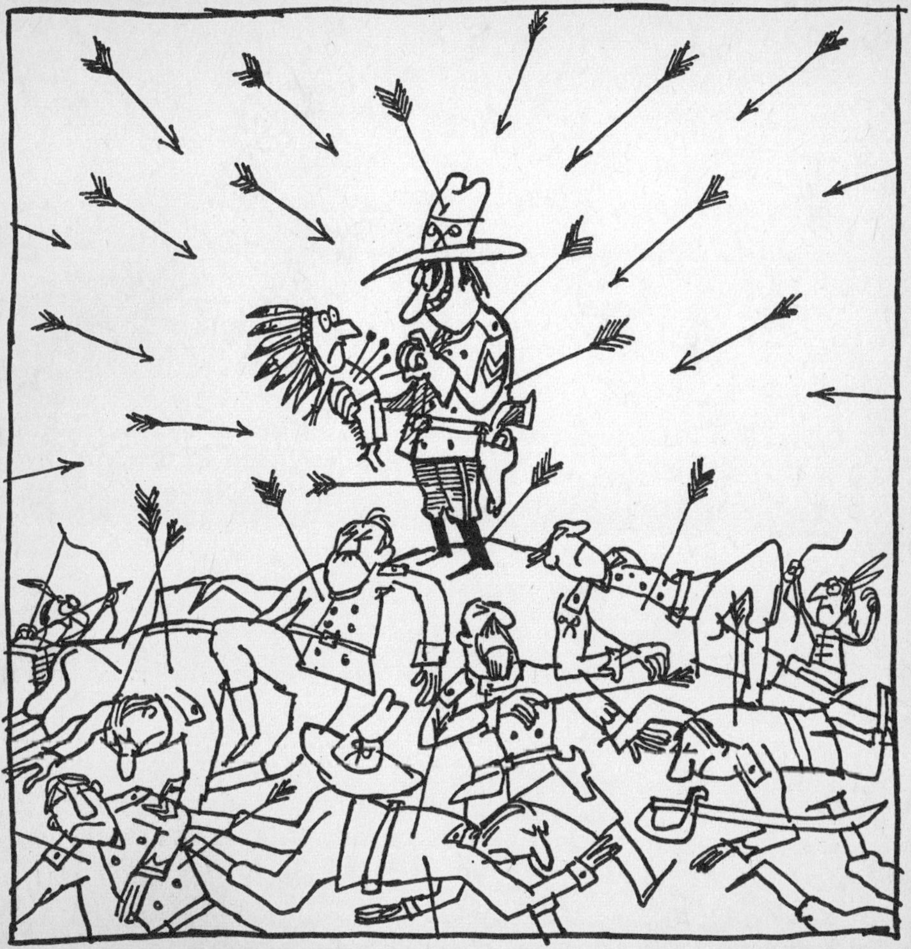

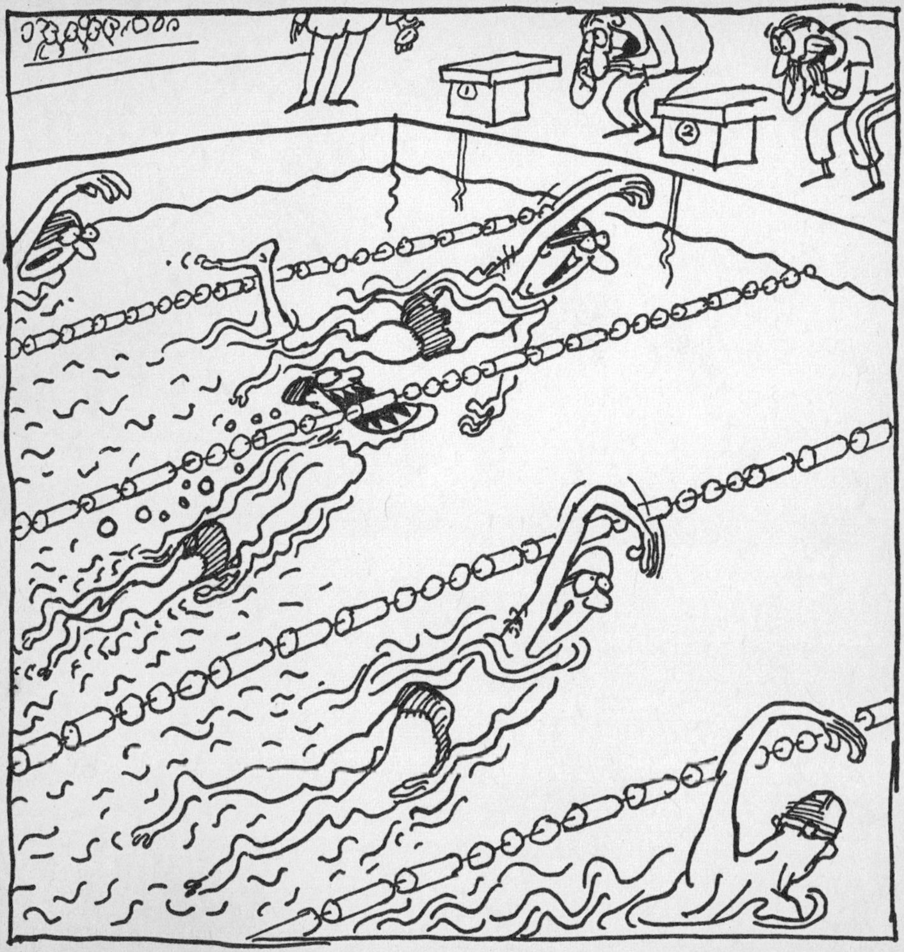
1
2

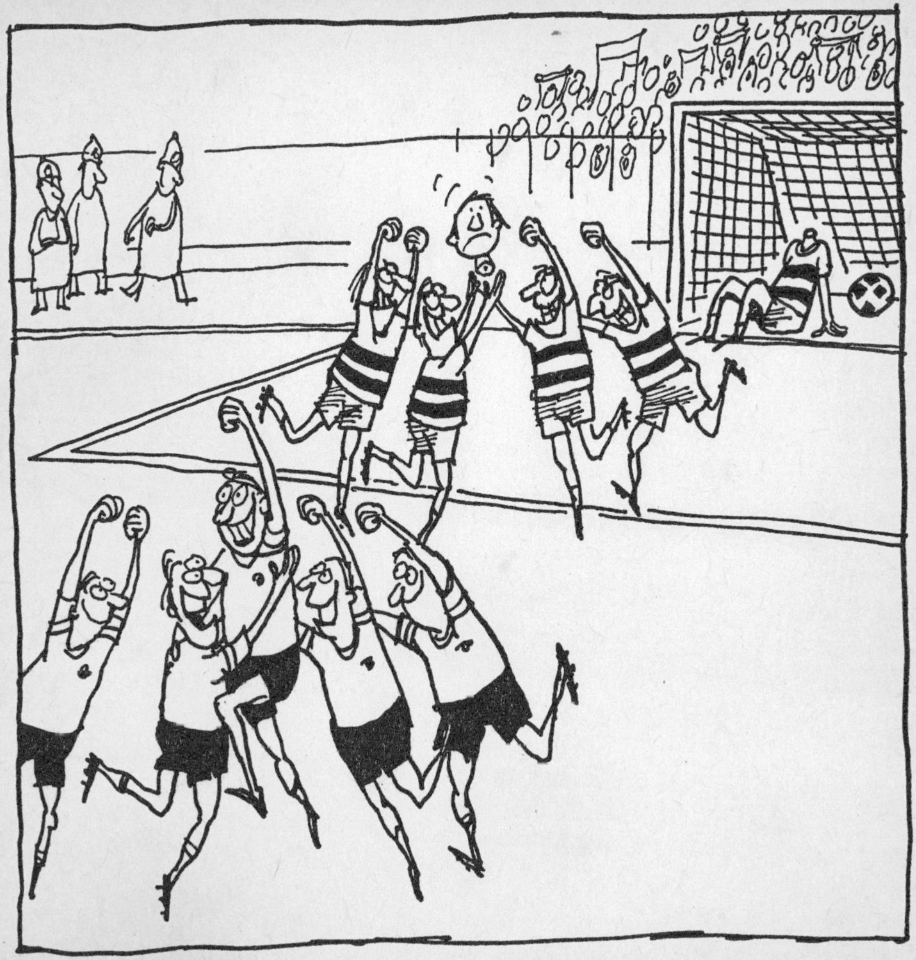

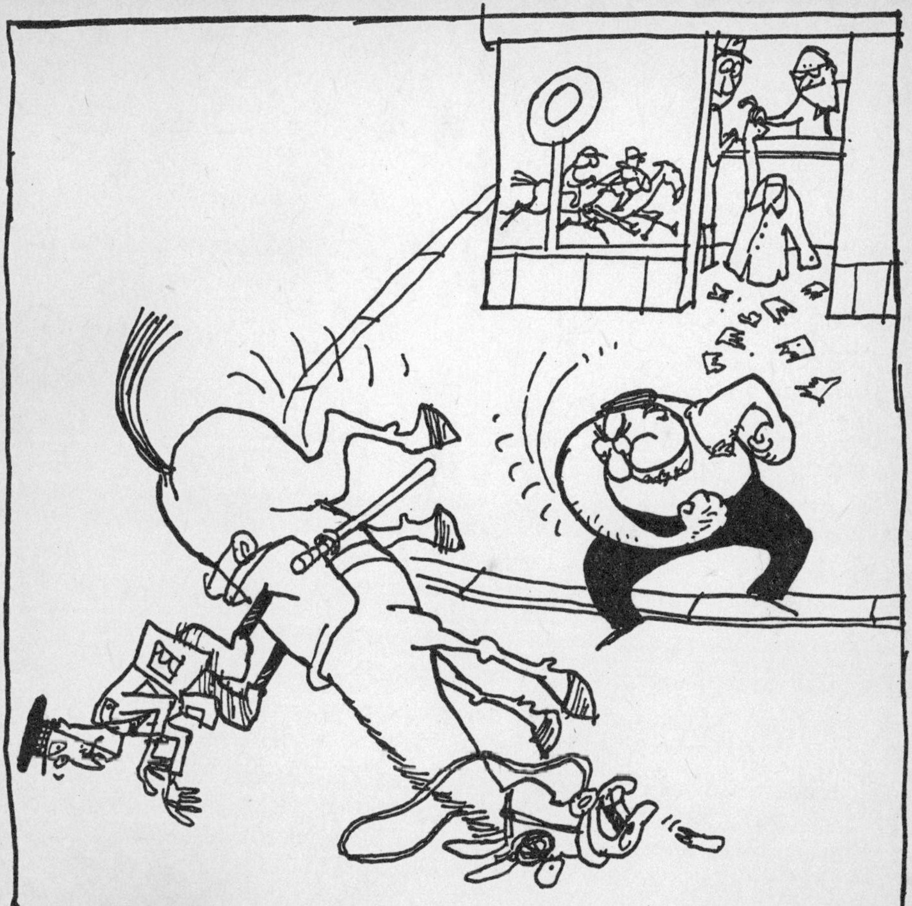

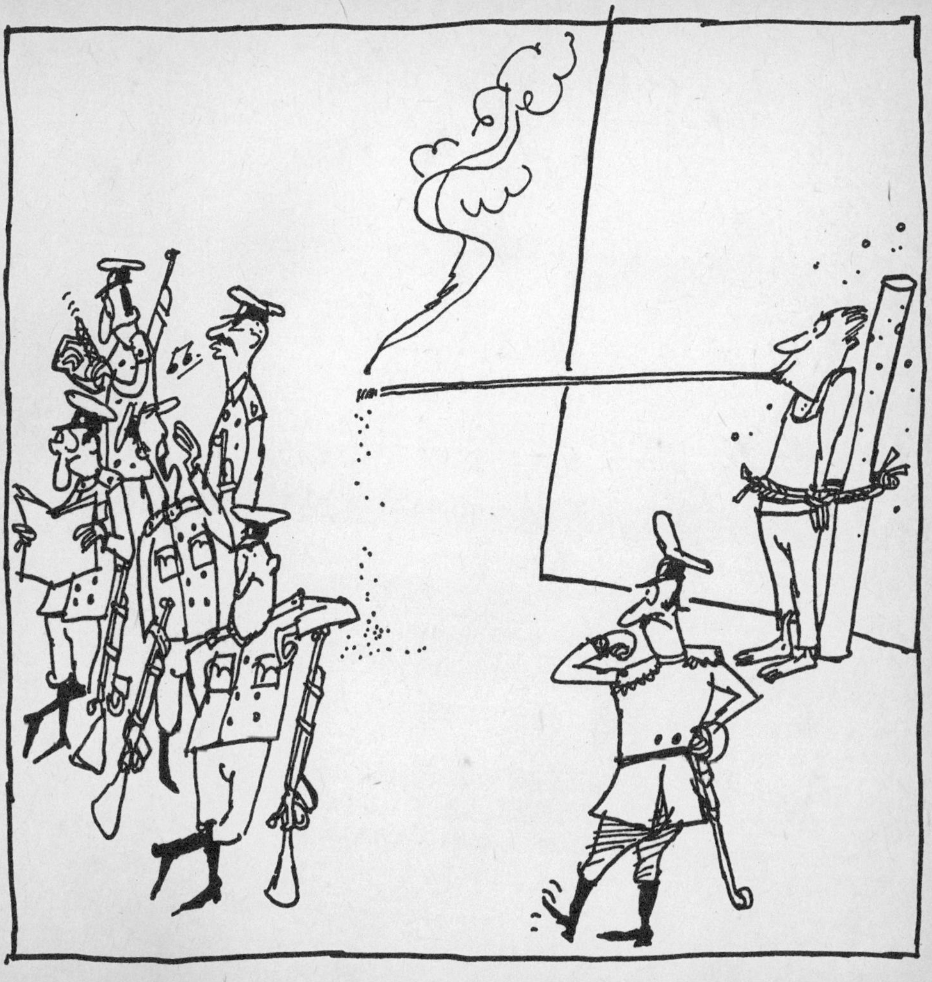

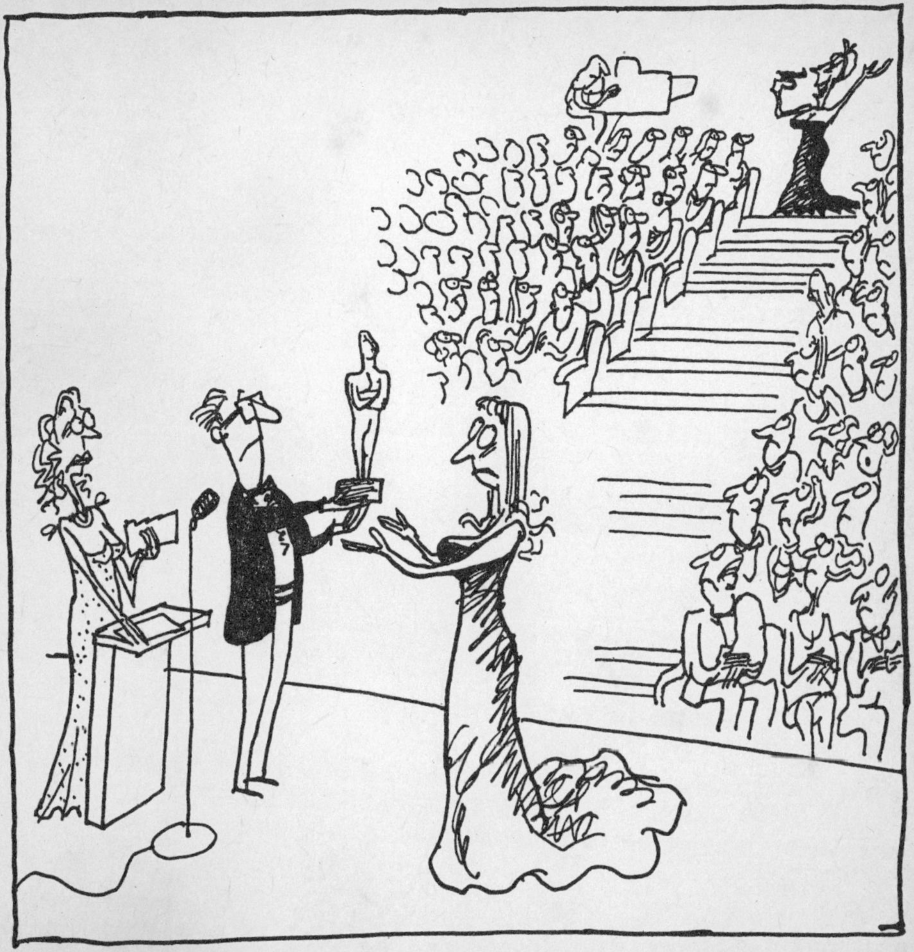

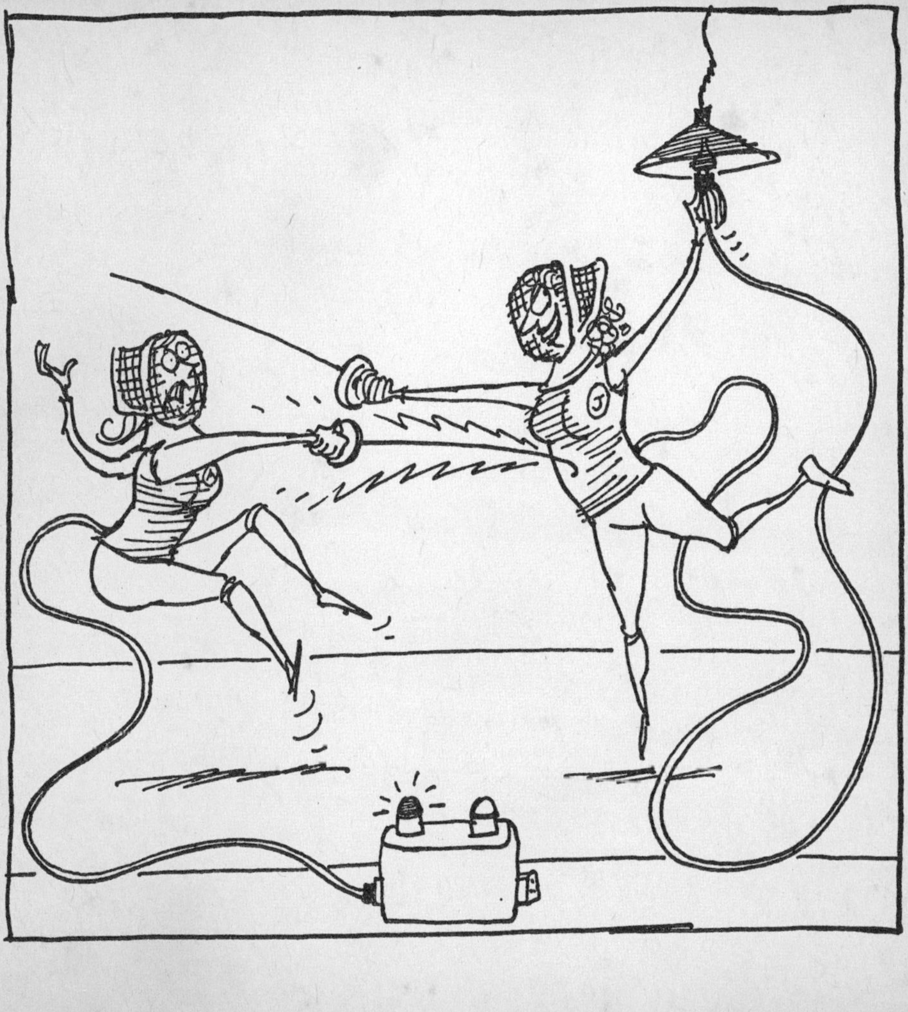

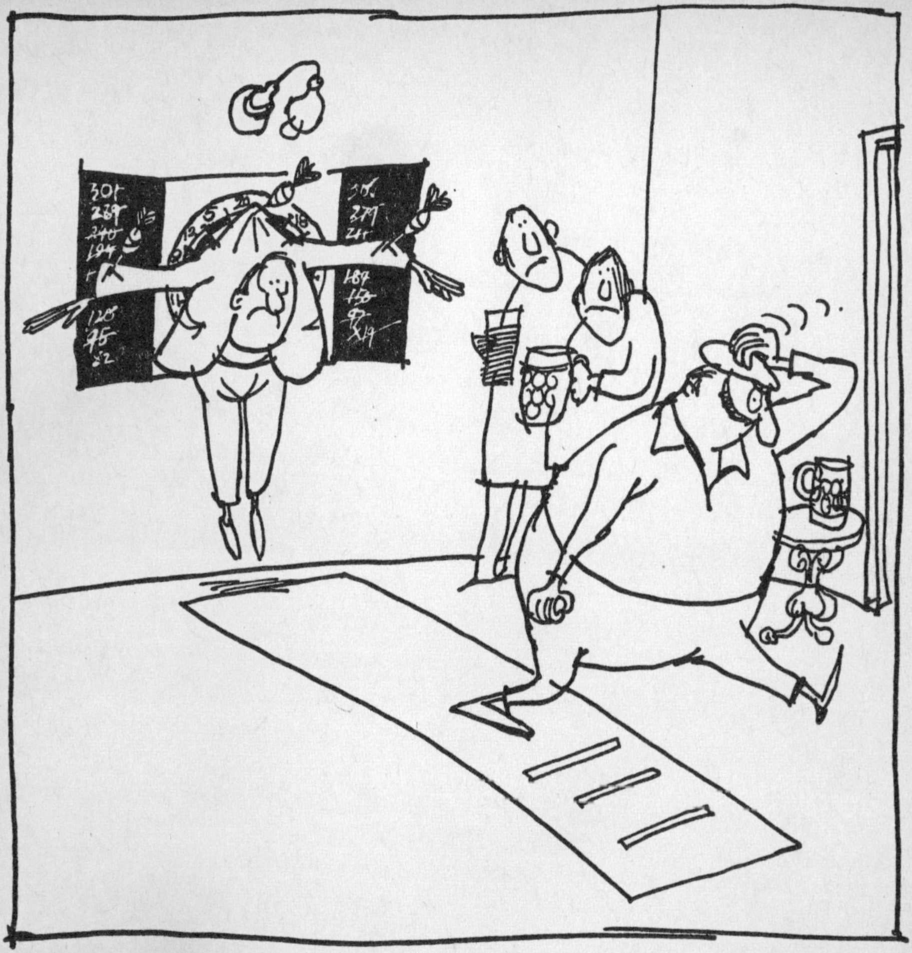

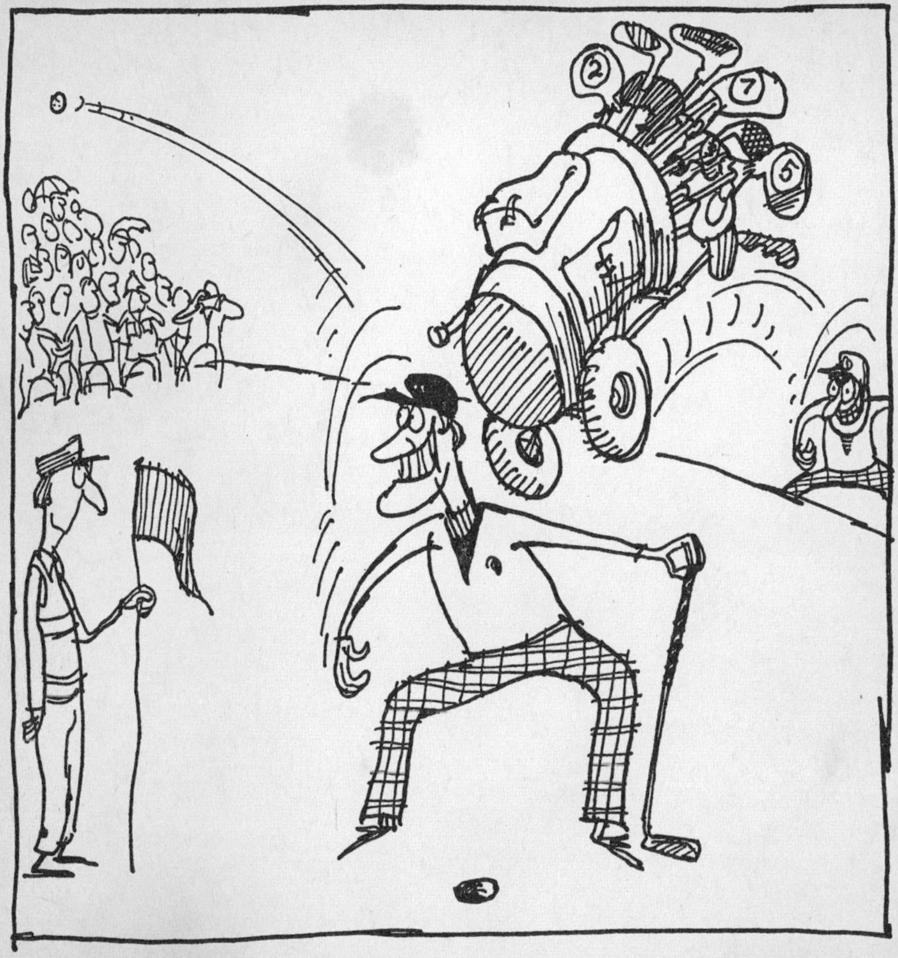

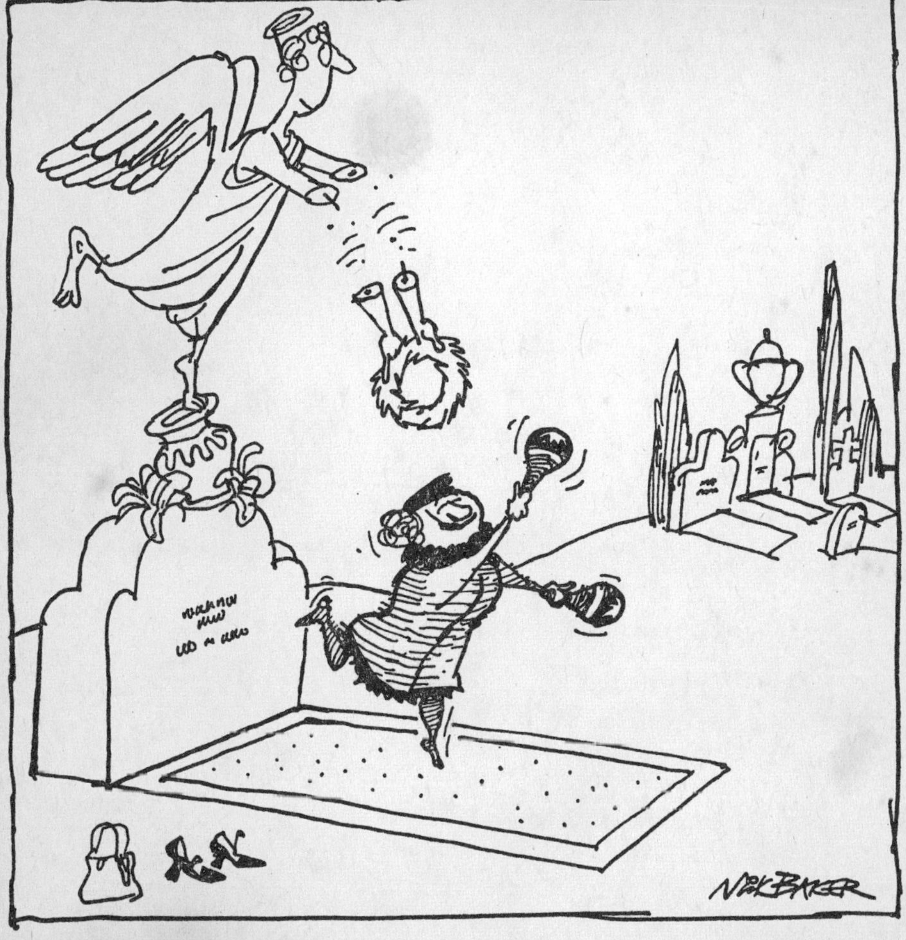
NICK BAKER